Give God the Glory!

The Godly Family Life

Other books in this series by Kevin Wayne Johnson:

Give God the Glory!
Know God & Do the Will of God Concerning *Your* Life
© 2001

Give God the Glory!
Called to be *Light* in the Workplace
© 2003

Give God the Glory!
Let Your *Light* So Shine- A Gift/Devotional Book
© 2004

Give God the Glory!

The Godly Family Life

Kevin Wayne Johnson

Writing for the Lord Ministries
Clarksville, Maryland 21029
www.writingforthelord.com

Give God the Glory! The Godly Family Life
© 2005 by Kevin Wayne Johnson, 1960 -
First Printing

Cover Concept by Kevin Wayne Johnson
Cover Design by Zendra Manley – The Mazzochi Group
Three Rivers, Michigan
1 (877) 842-6916

Distributed throughout the United States, Canada, and Europe by:

Faithworks, a Division of Send the Light, Ltd.
1 (877) 323-4550 / 1 (877) 323-4551 (fax)
www.faithworksonline.com (website)

Unless otherwise noted, all scripture references are taken from the King James Version of *The Holy Bible*, The New Open Bible Study Edition, Thomas Nelson, Incorporated, 1990. From time to time, I have added emphasis to scripture quotations by boldface type or all capitalization of certain words or phrases.

ISBN: 0-9705902-3-7
ISBN: 978-0-9705902-3-8

Library of Congress Catalog Number: 2005900305

Printed in the United States of America

Praise for *Give God the Glory!* The Godly Family Life:

This one may be the most compelling book yet! I have three sons and many spiritual and social sons that I have already promised in my heart to get a copy in their hands. The personal work sheets at the end of each chapter are a perfect personal accountability tool. I can see God changing the foundation of the family right before our eyes through the power of the words in this book. The use of scripture, real scriptural men, personal life experience and indisputable statistics appeal to whichever kind of scrutinizing eye through which we might read this material. My heart is racing at the lives that I personally envision will be changed! – *Paulette Holloway, Director, Bethany Christian Services, Crofton, Maryland*

Kevin Johnson hits the nail on the head with this book! This book is a wake up call to all men to assume their role as the head in the family and show them how. The principles taught in this book, if applied, will strengthen many families and serve as a guide to those who want to start successful families. I highly recommend this book. – *Reverend Ed Gray, author, "40 Days to a Life of G.O.L.D. (God Ordained Life Development)," Ed Gray Unlimited, Atlanta, Georgia*

Truly, the foundation of our world, the family, is under attack. The traditional family has been and is being re-defined by modern society. As fathers and mothers we must be willing to go to war to recapture and secure our God-given tour-of-duty of being effective parents. Kevin Wayne Johnson is like a general giving marching orders and challenging his troops/parents for the fight. Kevin Johnson's inspirational battle plans are boldly and clearly presented in his new book, *The Godly Family Life*. I highly recommend that all parents sign-up, re-enlist or even be drafted to review these battle plans and join in the fight for our families. TO GOD BE THE GLORY. GREAT THINGS HE HAS DONE. - *Dr. Larry Harris, author, "It*

All Starts at Home: 15 Ways to Put Family First,-"
Fayetteville, North Carolina www.ItAllStartsatHome.com

CONTENTS

PART II.

The Impact and Role of a Mother

PART III.

The Phases and Role of a Child

This book is dedicated to my loving family – my wife, Gail, and our three young sons, Kevin, Christopher, and Cameron. Second only to my love for my Heavenly Father, through Jesus Christ, my family brings an indescribable joy that sustains and fulfills me every day. It is only through the family unit that I can experience the genuine joy of being a husband and father. I love you and enjoy God's manifold blessings! *I thank God for you...*

Acknowledgments

I am sincerely thankful for the awesome opportunity to share my gift at a time in history that the family is under attack. First, I acknowledge my Heavenly Father, through Jesus Christ, as my source of strength, encouragement, wisdom, understanding, endurance, confidence, boldness, and biblical accuracy. Without Him, this book series would not be possible and they could not reach the thousands of readers, that they have reached, around the world.

I thank my late mom, and my dad, wife, and three sons for the family support, fun, and good times that we share daily. Your steadfast love keeps me going and going.

I thank the following professionals for their years of support with book marketing and promotion: Pam Perry, Delores Thornton, C&B Books Distributors, Larry Carpenter, Angela Rogers, Terry Owens, Marsha Sumner, Lawrence Wayne, Dr. Eugene Williams, Tanya Evans, Terri Hannett, Evelyn and Joseph Curtiss, Pastor L. and Mrs. Patricia Williams, Su Wood, Winston Chaney, Marilyn White, CMC Agents, Inc., the numerous bookstore managers that have hosted excellent book signing events, and all of the wonderful pastors across the country who graciously opened their doors and allowed me to introduce this book series to their respective congregations. I thank the multiple radio and television personalities for the opportunity to spread the gospel of Jesus Christ on the air - live or on tape.

I thank the following authors for their advice, counsel, and mentoring: Andria Hall, Minister Mary Edwards, Bishop Donald Downing, Yolanda Powell, Allison Gappa Bottke, Marlene Bagnull, Johnny Parker, and William and Selena Owens. Thank you, Zendra Manley, for another beautiful cover design that captures the essence of this book. Great job! Special thanks go to Pastor Robbie Davis and Bishop Robert Davis, Sr. at Celebration Church – *City of Champions* - for introducing this book to my wonderful readers with a powerful foreword. When we met in October 2004, I sensed the connection but did not know where it would lead us. God is good...all the time. Thank you, Steve Gilliland, for allowing God to use you as the spark that has since caught me on fire to *write for the lord.*

An especially grateful acknowledgement to all of my readers and supporters worldwide – thank you, thank you, thank you. Your loyalty and confidence in this book series encourages me to continue my personal ministry work in the Body of Christ. I thank you for your continued word-of-mouth support, for subscribing to the rapidly growing *Give God the Glory!* e-newsletter, and for viewing the *Give God the Glory!* weekly television show that is Web cast on www.blacktvonline.com, as the *Writing for the Lord* Ministries family continues to grow and prosper. To you, and everyone involved in this ministry project, I say THANK YOU!

Enjoy God's blessings...

Kevin Wayne Johnson

*"Now the LORD had said unto Abram, Get thee out of thy country, and from thy kindred, and from thy father's house, unto a land that I will shew thee: And I will make of thee a great nation, and I will bless thee, and make thy name great; and thou shalt be a blessing: And I will bless them that bless thee, and curse him that curseth thee: and in thee shall all **families** of the earth be blessed."*

(Genesis 12: 1 – 3)

FOREWORD

These are troubling times for the family, but thank God for the faithfulness of His Word and His promise in Luke 1:17, which states, "And he (John the Baptist) will go on before the Lord, in the spirit and power of Elijah, to turn the hearts of the fathers to their children and the disobedient to the wisdom of the righteous - to make ready a people prepared for the Lord" (NIV). Deacon Kevin Wayne Johnson is one of the faithful men being used of God to sound a distinct call for men, fathers, and families to focus their attention on the dire needs of their families.

The enemy, the adversary of God, Satan has been successful in many instances with millions upon of millions of men the world over, but especially here in our country and our communities, turning the hearts of men away from their children, their wives and their churches and, in turn, have turned them to focusing on their own, what many are thinking is a hopeless condition. In this book, Deacon Johnson has very skillfully pointed men and women, boys and girls to the One who is the true source for healing and deliverance in our land.

It is sad to say, there are too many homes headed by single female parents, thus creating a huge "father-hunger" in our culture. Hence, there is an intense need to see God disclose Himself as "Abba Father." Many fathers are unable to relate properly to their families because they have never had the model of their own father acted out properly before them. There are hurting, aching and struggling men, fathers with their own children and wives, because of the bitterness they have from their early days of absent fathers. The role of father and mother has been beautifully presented in this book as God's plan has been laid out in His Word, the Bible. Kevin Wayne Johnson is teaching us clearly and deliberately to "Give God the Glory!"

This is not only a manual that is full of very insightful information for fathers and mothers, men, women and children, but can also be useful as a devotional guide. God is using Deacon Johnson powerfully as He used Elijah and John the Baptist, "to turn the hearts of the fathers to their children and the disobedient to the wisdom of the righteous - to make ready a people prepared for the Lord."

Bishop Robert S. Davis, Sr.

Covering Bishop
Celebration Church...*City of Champions*
Columbia, Maryland

Preface

I write this book at a time in history when the family is under attack at an unprecedented rate.

The first-ever rating of prime television's portrayal of fatherhood was in 1999. It concluded that few fathers are to be found on prime-time television and those that are, usually are portrayed as incompetent or detached. Of the 102 shows originally reviewed, only 15, or 14.7%, featured a father who has children under the age of eighteen as a recurring central character. This study, conducted by the National Fatherhood Initiative, reviewed prime-time television on the five major networks from mid-November through mid-December, 1998.

With each generation, a myriad of facts reveal the deterioration of the family unit. Its current state is in a crisis mode, but has society considered what God has to say about it? A Supreme Court decision on January 22, 1973 – *Roe vs. Wade* – is partly attributable to the more than 40 million abortions performed in America since that time. That decision ruled that the right to personal property *includes* abortion. The USA Today newspaper ran a cover story on the front page on May 2, 2005 titled, *"The Changing Politics of Abortion."* The essence of the story centered on how political leaders voted relative to abortion rights – Is it or is it not legal to abort a child? Up to forty-five percent of Republican lawmakers polled agree that abortion is legal in a few circumstances. However, the middle verse of *The Holy Bible* teaches us that *"It is better to trust in the LORD than to put confidence in man"* (Psalm 118:8).

U.S. News & World Report featured a special report on May 24, 2004, *"The Rise of the Gay Family,"* highlighting that more and more American children are growing up with same-sex parents. Although this was not a cover story in this issue, its contents were spread prominently throughout five pages, and labeled as a "special" report, garnering as much attention as the cover story of the week. In the August 2004 issue of *The Vine*, an Upper Marlboro, Maryland-based Christian newspaper, the cover story highlighted the anniversary of homosexual Bishop Vicki Gene Robinson's confirmation hearing. He was the first openly reported homosexual bishop in the Episcopal Church USA. Also, reportedly, there are 40,000 new HIV infections each year.

Lastly, 24 million children (34 percent) live absent their biological father and these children are, on average, at least two to three times more likely to be poor, to use drugs, to experience educational, health, emotional and behavioral problems, to be victims of child abuse, and to engage in criminal behavior than their peers who live with their married (biological or adoptive) parents. How has this affected you personally? What happened?

God's plan for the family is so important that He references *family* or *families* in *The Holy Bible* 285 times! Moreover, references to father, mother, and child, and their variations, are found 963, 325, and 1,957 times, respectively! In the first book of *The Holy Bible*, God reveals unto Abram "*...in thee shall all families of the earth be blessed"* (Genesis 12: 1-3).

So why has the world disregarded God's instructions pertaining to the family? I wanted to know why, so I studied, researched, prayed, observed, listened, read extensively, traveled, and wrote. This is book #4 in the *Give God the Glory!* series of books and devotionals. Let's explore, together, what God's plan was, and still is, for His family.

Together, let's *Give God the Glory!*

Introduction

"Honour thy father and thy mother: that thy days may be long upon the land which the LORD thy God giveth thee."
(Exodus 20:12)

"HONOUR THY FATHER AND MOTHER; which is the first commandment with promise. THAT IT MAY BE WELL WITH THEE, AND THOU MAYEST LIVE LONG ON THE EARTH."
(Ephesians 6:2-3)

God's first commandment to man, with a promise, deals with the *family*. Holiness in *family life* is evident in the Apostle Paul's teaching to the saints and faithful brethren in Christ (Colossians 1:2). In this dynamic teaching, God's Word clearly reveals His plans, roles, and responsibilities for the family that He created.

- Wives *"...submit yourselves unto your **own** husbands, **as it is fit in the Lord**"* (Colossians 3:18).

- Husbands *"...love **your** wives, and be not bitter against them"* (Colossians 3:19).

- Children *"...obey your parents in **all** things: for this is **well pleasing unto the Lord**"* (Colossians 3:20).

1

- Fathers   *"...provoke not your children to anger, lest they be discouraged"* (Colossians 3:21).

The consistent nature of God's Word is again illuminated through the Apostle Paul's teaching to the saints and faithful in Christ Jesus at Ephesus (Ephesians 1:1) relative to holiness in family life. In several powerful passages of Scripture, beginning in chapter 5, verse 21, through chapter 6, verse 4, God Word's comforts His readers with a detailed focus on the believer's responsibility to walk in accordance with their heavenly calling in Christ Jesus. In essence, this is the *key* to the book of Ephesians: That we become more aware of our position in Christ because this is the basis for our practice on every level of life.

- Wives   *"...submit yourselves unto your **own** husbands, **as unto the Lord**"* (Ephesians 5:22)"*...as the church is subject unto Christ, so let the wives be to their **own** husbands in every thing"* (Ephesians 5:24).

- Husbands   *"...**love your wives**, even as Christ also loved the church, and gave Himself for it"* (Ephesians 5:25)"*...so ought men to **love their wives** as their own bodies. **He that loveth his wife loveth himself**"* (Ephesians 5:28).

- Marriage   *"For this cause SHALL A MAN LEAVE HIS FATHER AND MOTHER, AND SHALL BE JOINED UNTO THIS WIFE, AND*

2

THEY TWO SHALL BE ONE FLESH"
(Ephesians 5:31).

- Husband and Wife   *"...let everyone of you in particular so **love his wife even as himself**; and the **wife see that she reverence her husband**"* (Ephesians 5:33).

- Children   *"...**obey** your parents in the Lord: for this is right. **HONOUR** THY FATHER AND MOTHER; which is the first commandment with promise; THAT IT MAY BE WELL WITH THEE, AND THOU MAYEST LIVE LONG ON THE EARTH"* (Ephesians 6:1-3).

God's Plan for the Family

Simply put, the family centers around mom and dad. It means:

Father

And

Mother

I

Love

You

"It's Christmas!," my middle son shouted at 7:13am on December 25th. As his two brothers and mother slept, he made his way to the living room, from his bedroom, to open his toys with great anticipation. I exploded with

3

gladness knowing that my family would be fulfilled on this day.

The celebration of Christmas Day brings such joy to my heart. It is one of the more special times to teach my family about Jesus. It is His birth that is first and foremost on my mind during this season. No time to discuss Santa Claus, no time to get too caught up in secular Christmas songs, and no time to spend countless hours in stores making others rich. Instead, this time of the year is appropriate for family to spend quality time together celebrating the new life that we have because of the love that God has for us – His children. This is a time to get away from the daily rigor and chaos of life and take the time to:

- Talk,
- Celebrate,
- Love,
- Cherish memories,
- Hug,
- Cry,
- Pray,
- Restore,
- Reflect,
- Rest,
- Relax, and
- Pray.

God's first commandment, which is sealed with a *promise*, centers on the *family* and family life. This is revealed twice in the Old Testament (Exodus 20:12 – one of the original Ten Commandments – and again in Deuteronomy 5:16). The New Testament revelation is written as follows:

> *"HONOUR THY FATHER AND MOTHER; which is the first commandment with promise. THAT IT MAY BE WELL WITH THEE, AND THOU MAYEST LIVE LONG ON THE EARTH."*
> (Ephesians 6:2-3)

F-A-M-I-L-Y is mentioned 123 times in *The Holy Bible* – 122 in the Old Testament and once in the New Testament. In its original form, in the Greek language – *patria* – it means "an ancestry, lineage, family or tribe." Another translation – *oikos* – means "a household, family, a dwelling, a house." With dads taking the lead, develop a close and intimate relationship with your family as follows:

1. Make the things of God a priority in your life. Live by the Word, do the Word, and seek the kingdom of God first, above all issues and concerns in your life. God promises to take care of you with the natural needs (food, clothing, and shelter) that are essential to survival in this world. Submit yourself to Him.

> *"But seek ye first the kingdom of God, and His righteousness; and all these things shall be added unto you."*

(Matthew 6:33)

5

"Submit yourselves therefore to God. Resist the devil, and he will flee from you."

(James 4:7)

2.   Become a <u>prayer warrior</u>. Talk to God on behalf of your FAMILY. Communicate with Him. He desires to talk to His children. It takes practice but will soon become a normal part of your day. Morning devotionals must become a priority. Men are to be the natural example in our homes.

"Confess your faults one to another, and pray one for another, that ye may be healed. The effectual fervent prayer of a righteous man availeth much."

(James 5:16)

"Ye have not chosen me, but I have chosen you, and ordained you, that ye should go and bring forth fruit, and that your fruit should remain: that whatsoever ye shall ask of the Father in my name, he may give it you."

(John 15:16)

3.   Make God clear and visible. Read and study God's Word at least five to six hours per week. Then, do what the Word says to do.

"And, I if I be lifted up from the earth, will draw all men unto me."

(John 12:32)

*"Ye are the **salt** of the earth: but if the **salt** have lost his savour, wherewith shall it be salted? It is thenceforth good for nothing, but to be cast out, and to be trodden under foot of men. Ye are the **light** of the world. A city that is set on an hill cannot be hid. Neither do men **light** a candle, and put it under a bushel, but on a candlestick; and it giveth **light** unto all that are in the house. Let your **light** so shine before men, that they may see your good works, and glorify your Father which is in heaven."*
(Matthew 5:13-16)

Salt – Cleanses, purifies, seasons, and disinfects.

Light – Exposes darkness, penetrates, leads, guides, directs, expels corruption, radiates, and shines!

4.   Spend quality time together.

"Can two walk together, except they be agreed?"

(Amos 3:3)

"And thou shalt love the LORD thy God with all thine heart, and with all thy soul, and with all thy might. And these words, which I command thee this day, shall be in thine heart; And thou shalt teach them diligently unto thy children, and shalt talk of them when thou sitteth in thine house, and when thou walkest by the way, and when thou liest down, and when thou riseth up."

(Deuteronomy 6:5-7)

"...when thou sitteth in thine house" – teach the children about the LORD our God at all times. Do not allow anything in

your home that will distract their ways, their thinking, or their habits. Shut off HBO, avoid the music videos, and monitor their Internet usage.

"...when thou walkest by the way" – Take the time to walk them to school and attend their recreational activities as a chaperone, coach or volunteer.

"...when thou liest down and when thou riseth up" – Be the last one to go to bed at night and the first one to rise in the morning. Be at home both at night and in the morning for your children.

5.   Learn from one another.

> *"To know wisdom and instruction; to perceive the words of understanding; To receive the instruction of wisdom, justice, and judgment, and equity; To give subtlety to the simple, to the young man knowledge and discretion. A wise man will hear; and will increase learning; and a man of understanding shall attain unto wise counsels: To understand a proverb, and the interpretation; the words of the wise, and their dark sayings. The fear of the LORD is the beginning of knowledge: but fools despise wisdom and instruction."*

(Proverbs 1:2-7)

6.   Walk by faith, not by sight.

> *"Even so faith, if it hath not works, is dead, being alone."*

(James 2:17)

"For we walk by faith, not by sight."

(2 Corinthians 5:7)

7.   Allow the love of God to shine in your hearts. Follow the lead of Joshua – the ultimate family man.

"This book of the law shall not depart out of thy mouth: but thou shalt meditate therein day and night, that thou mayest observe to do according to all that is written therein: for then thou shalt make thy way prosperous, and then thou shalt have good success."

(Joshua 1:8)

This family man succeeded Moses and his capable leadership survived three military campaigns involving more than thirty enemy armies. Ultimately, though, victory comes through faith in God and obedience to His Word rather than through military might or numerical superiority.

Make a new commitment to live according to God's plan for family as a result of reading and sharing this book. Make a renewed commitment to spend quality time with your family. Remember what family means:

(**F**)ather (**A**)nd (**M**)other (**I**) (**L**)ove (**Y**)ou!   Let your love extend to your family. Our children need us.

Part I.

The Significance and Role of a Father

"And, ye fathers, provoke not your children to wrath; but bring them up in the nurture and admonition of the Lord."

(Ephesians 6:4)

11

Character

Integrity

Ethical

Unashamed of the Gospel

A leader

Decision-Maker

Loves His Family

Cherishes His Wife

Raises His Children in the Fear of the Lord

Responsible in All Facets of Life

Well-Groomed

Respectful

Excellence of Ministry

From an historical perspective, man established a special day to acknowledge and recognize the "role" of fatherhood. This day, of all days, fathers are to be celebrated. This is a fairly new phenomenon in today's culture relative to timing. Here is the story of Father's Day:

Mrs. John B. Dodd, of Washington, first proposed the idea of a "father's day" in 1909. Mrs. Dodd wanted a special day to honor her father, William Smart. William Smart, a Civil War veteran, was widowed when his wife (Mrs. Dodd's mother) died in childbirth with their sixth child. Mr. Smart was left to raise the newborn and his other five children by himself on a rural farm in eastern Washington State. It was after Mrs. Dodd became an adult that she realized the strength and selflessness her father had shown in raising his children as a single parent.

The first Father's Day was observed on June 19, 1910 in Spokane, Washington. At about the same time in various towns and cities across American other people were beginning to celebrate a "father's day." In 1924 President Calvin Coolidge supported the idea of a national Father's Day. Finally, in 1966, President Lyndon Johnson signed a presidential proclamation declaring the third Sunday of June as Father's Day.

Father's Day has become a day to not only honor your father, but all men who act as a father figure. Stepfathers, uncles, grandfathers, and adult male friends are all honored on Father's Day.

God's perspective is quite different. He created man is *His* image, after *His* likeness, and gave him (man) dominion over all the earth (Genesis 1:26). He did not stop there. God inspected all that He had made and declared it was *very good* (Genesis 1:31). Throughout *The Holy Bible,* there are over 900 references to *father* and four other variations. *Father*, a noun, derives from the Greek word – *patēr* – meaning "a nourisher, protector, and upholder." This word, in its singular form, is used 963 times. Other forms of this word include:

> ➤ fathers – 522 times,
> ➤ father's - 146 times,
> ➤ fathers' – 10 times, and
> ➤ fatherless – 41times.

Additionally, there are 254 references to the Heavenly Father (God Almighty) throughout the Scriptures. Fatherhood, then, is an awesome role, responsibility, and duty in the overall plan of God for mankind.

While we applaud man's attempts to acknowledge fathers' on a special day, God has already ordained the role of fatherhood. A man's role in this regard is much more significant than society realizes or can comprehend. To

14

this end, Part I will repeatedly emphasize what the Apostle Peter preached to the Council in the Books of Acts, "...*we ought to obey God rather than men* (Acts 5:29)." If we follow God's Word, we cannot help but succeed in our homes, work-places, schools, and churches.

Chapter One

The Family Man

"...but as for me and my house, we will serve the Lord."
(Joshua 24:15)

"'The Family Man'" [1] is a sermon that has been taught twice by my former pastor over the past fifteen years. I feel compelled to share bits and pieces of this moving series through this article. I live what I write and I have a call on my life to impact the lives of the male seed, both young and old.

It is worth noting that the man is the foundation of the family, the family is the foundation of the local church, and the local church(s) is the foundation of the Body of Christ. Joshua clearly demonstrated, through his leadership to the people of Israel and as a family man, that victory comes through faith in God and obedience to His Word. Joshua (Hebrew equivalent to the Greek name Iesous – Jesus) was born a slave in Egypt, yet became a conqueror in Canaan.

17

He was a personal assistant to Moses and, later, his successor. The entire Book of Joshua describes the entering, conquering, and occupying of the land of Canaan. Joshua, as a family man, was able to accomplish three significant things during his lifetime:

1. He took a position for himself.
2. He took a position for his family.

3. He took a position for the people of Israel.

By his example, Joshua's life teaches men the following:

Be a Living Epistle

Joshua...the son of Nun. Although there is nothing specifically mentioned about Nun in *The Holy Bible*, Joshua is frequently identified by God as the *son of Nun*. This signifies that he lived a life patterned after his father, Nun. He became what his natural father taught him. Men must become what our Heavenly Father teaches us in our ordained roles as fathers.

Have a Godly Attitude

In the Book of Matthew, chapter 5, verses 3 through 10, Jesus teaches His first public sermon during His three-and-a-half year earthly ministry. The first principles that Jesus teaches His disciples and the multitudes are the BEATITUDES – *the attitude we ought to be*. That is, humility, meekness (power under control), to hunger after righteousness, to be mournful at the pitiful condition of this world, merciful, do good and expect good intentions, and to make peace.

Fears the Lord

In Proverbs 1:7, God teaches us that *"The fear of the LORD is the beginning of knowledge...."* Knowledge is a key element of our Christian walk. It is fundamental to our success as men, husbands, and fathers.

Has Godly Character   ...a servant's heart

The family man demonstrates his Godly character:

- with love: willing to sacrifice
- with his attitude: shapes the personality of his home.
- with hope: fully expects to receive for his family because hope does not disappoint.
- with his "'substance'": places his family first. The family man makes God clear and visible at home.

Has a Courageous Heart

A courageous man has the utmost confidence in what God says, and ACTS UPON IT!

Spiritual Vision

A family man with spiritual vision is able to "'*see*'" what God said concerning his family.

Acknowledges Responsibility

Responsibility breeds accountability. A family man CHOOSES to accept responsibility for the overall well being of his family.

Accepts Responsibility

The family is an institution established by God. It is the family man's responsibility to raise the children. Our righteousness can and will save the family.

Is a Leader

To be an effective leader, we must have personal experiences with God. In Numbers 27:18-23, *The Holy Bible* gives a detailed account of Moses' successor, Joshua. Both men had experiences with God that verified their fitness to lead.

Set Under Authority

In Hebrews 5:8, Jesus stayed under the authority of the Word of His Heavenly Father, through obedience.

Receives Instructions and Follows Instructions

- In Victory: without full understanding.
- In Defeat: even in defeat, a family man does not abandon his family.

Joshua's life is one that men should emulate. He is the ultimate family man. Study his life, watch his actions, examine his motives, observe his study patterns as he learned from Moses, view his tenacity, and learn from his leadership.

I am a family man. My family and I will serve the Lord. Looking to Joshua as my example, and based upon what I have learned in this chapter, we will serve the Lord together in the following ways:

1.

_____

2.

_____

3.

_____

4.

_____

5.

_____

Chapter Two

How Do I Carry Out God's Plan for Fathers?

"Wise men lay up knowledge: but the mouth of the foolish is near destruction."
(Proverbs 10:14)

You were formed for God's family. God wants a family, and He created you to be a part of it. This is God's second purpose for your life, which He planned before you were born.[2] It is really important that we really understand that God created man for the purpose of establishing a family with whom He could fellowship. Unfortunately, man has been negligent in fulfilling the purpose for which God created.[3] To successfully carry out our ordained role as

23

fathers, in accordance with God's plan for our lives, we must regularly study the Scriptures as it relates to *nourishing, protecting, and upholding* our children.

During our study, I encourage all fathers to focus and mediate upon Jesus' first public sermon before his disciples and the multitude – the Sermon on the Mount – during His three-and-a-half year earthly ministry. From His teachings, there are four key elements that can be extracted from this powerful message of hope that we must be committed to and actively pursue: Seek first the Kingdom of God, let *your* light shine, demonstrate love, and maintain (or live) a fervent prayer life.

a.   *"Seek ye first the kingdom of God, and His righteousness; and all these things shall be added unto you"* (Matthew 6:33).

Always seek God first and foremost in every area of your life. He will add to your life all that you need to care for your children – housing, food, and clothing. Especially seek His righteousness, and the blessings that will cover your family will come through you first as the head. Care for your children as God cares for us – His children.

b.   *"Let your light so shine before men, that they may see your good works, and glorify your Father which is in heaven"* (Matthew 5:16).

Your light in your home should radiate, illuminate, reflect, project, promote growth, and expel darkness. Be the visible image of God that your children can *see* in their daily walk. As light, you will also cause other men to be the fathers that God called them to be.

c. *"Be ye therefore perfect, even as your Father which is in heaven is perfect"* (Matthew 5:48).

The word *perfect* denotes "'mature.'" It takes a mature Christian to love unconditionally. The love of Jesus is unconditional. It takes unconditional love to be the father that God has called us to be. To love, protect, nurture, nourish, and uphold requires an unconditional love that can only come from God. This outward demonstration of love to enemies and, neighbors, as well as our children, speaks volumes. Love is a lifestyle that transcends the evil of this world, and our children will demonstrate the same attribute when they can see that it works. Love never fails.

d. *The Lord's Prayer* (Matthew 6:9-13).

Daily prayer is so important in the life of the Christian. Our Heavenly Father knows what we need before we ask (verse 8). The Lord's Prayer is a pattern of prayer that Jesus taught Himself. Prayer in the life of the true believer is an act of total confidence and assurance in the plan and purpose of God. God's plan for us as fathers can be revealed each time that we pray. Rely totally upon God, through Jesus Christ, to help in the time of need. I challenge all fathers to ask our Heavenly Father for guidance concerning our divine role. When – not if - the answer is provided, act upon it and enjoy the results!

Be a father as God intended for you to be. God will surely smile upon you, and the blessings upon your family will come through you as their conduit and as the head of your household. YOU ARE A FATHER. Love your ordained role (1 Corinthians 11:3) and be fulfilled while doing it!

Heavenly Father, in the name of Jesus, I desire to carry out your plan for my life. As a father, I will commit to do the following as a result of what I have learned from this chapter:

1. _____

2. _____

3. _____

4. _____

5. _____

Chapter Three

Attitudes About Fatherhood and Fatherlessness

"For the husband is the head of the wife, even as Christ is the head of the church: and he is the savior of the body. Therefore as the church is subject unto Christ, so let the wives be to their own husbands in every thing. Husbands, love your wives, even as Christ also loved the church, and gave himself for it, That he might present it to himself a glorious church, not having spot, or wrinkle, or any such thing; but that it should be holy and without blemish. So ought men to love their wives as their own bodies. He that loveth his wife loveth himself."
(Ephesians 5:23-28)

"The physical absence of the father from the home is the most significant problem facing America." – 72.2% of those polled in 1999 by a survey conducted by the Gallup Organization for the National Center for Fathering

"85% of adults say that the number of children being born to single parents is either a "serious" or "critical" social problem." – Roper Starch Worldwide, as reported in *Parenting*, November 1998.

As stated, the father is the *foundation* of the family. The family is the *foundation* of the church. The church is

29

the *foundation* of the Body of Christ. The church is to change the nation from unrighteousness to righteousness. The church is to make God *clear and visible* to the unbeliever.

The facts below are key statistics extracted from *"Father Facts, 4th Edition,"* a book published through the National Fatherhood Initiative, Gaithersburg, Maryland. As you will see from the statistics that have been reported, the foundation of the family is on shaky ground. I intend to give us a wake-up call as it relates to these statistics and cause us to ask ourselves the challenging question, "What am I going to do about it?" Attitudes about fatherhood and fatherlessness are derived from the following areas that affect the lives of children:

Father Absence

Of the 72 million children under 18 years old living in the U.S., 27 percent (19.2 million) were living with a single parent, and 4 percent (3 million) were living with neither parent. In America, 24 million children (34 percent) live absent their biological father.

Single-Parent Families

The number of children living in single-parent families rose from 5,829,000 in 1960 to 19,220,000 in 2000.

Out-of-Wedlock Childbearing

One out of every three children born in 2000 (33.1 percent) was born to unmarried parents. Amongst African-

Americans, the numbers grew from 49,200 (16.8 percent) in 1940 to 425,000 (68.5 percent) in 2000.

Divorce

The total number of divorces has increased steadily since 1960, from 390,000 to 1,135,000 in 1998. About 3 out of 5 divorcing couples have at least one child. Amongst the church and religious denominations, the percentage of adults who have been divorced are: Non-denominational (small groups) – 34%; Baptists – 29%; Mainline Protestants – 25%; Mormons – 24%; Catholics – 21%; and Lutherans – 21%.

Child Custody

Of the 14.0 million single, custodial parents in 1997, 11.9 million (85%) were mothers and 2.1 million (15%) were fathers.

Stepfamilies

Stepfamilies report greater levels of family tension and disagreement in their family relationships and lower levels of family cohesiveness and adaptability, compared to first-married families. Further, five to seven years after remarriage, stepfamilies continue to report less positive wife-to-husband and biological parent-child interactions compared to first-married families.

Cohabitation

Society accepts it; God's Word forbids it!

Non-Resident Fathers

Only a third of non-resident fathers are supporting new families that include children. The farther away a non-resident father lives from his children, the less likely he is to pay child support, visit his children, or show an interest in parental decision making.

Unwed Fathers

Using data from the Child Supplement to the National Longitudinal Survey of Youth, it was found that only 33% of unwed fathers were living with their children during the first year of the child's life. Of the 40% who were visiting their children during the first year of life, less than half continued to do so two years later.

Teen Fathers

Teenage fathers are more likely than their childless peers to commit and be convicted of illegal activity, and their offenses are of a more serious nature.

Incarcerated Fathers

In 1999, State and Federal prisons held an estimated 667,900 fathers of minor children, 44 percent of whom lived with their children prior to incarceration. 1,371,700 minor children currently have a father in State or Federal prison, an increase of 58 percent since 1991. Further, 10 million children have parents who have been imprisoned at some time in their lives.

Single Fatherhood

Single fathers comprise 17 percent – one out of every six – of the nation's 11.7 million single parents.

The central theme of this chapter about attitudes is for men to get, and stay, involved in the lives of our children – both boys and girls! They need us. God has entrusted us! Let's not disappoint the children and let's especially not abuse the trust that God has in us. Furthermore, love your wives. They *are* our glory. Love them as Christ loved the church...

Starting today, I will renew my mind with God's Word and change my attitude concerning my responsibilities as a father. I will be a Godly father figure to all children, not just my own, so that God is clear and visible to everyone that I come in contact with. Based upon what I have learned in this chapter, I will accomplish this in the following ways:

1.

_____

2.

_____

3.

_____

4.

_____

5.

_____

Chapter Four

Daddy, What a Precious Word!

"A man shall be satisfied with good by the fruit of his mouth:
and the recompense of a man's hands shall be rendered unto
him."
(Proverbs 12:14)

"Daddy, daddy, welcome home!" are the words that I hear almost everyday from my sons as I arrive home from a hard day's work. "Glad to see you, Daddy!" they say with such joy and tenderness of heart. I cannot explain in words how proud that makes me feel. Nor can I write through this book about the shear delight as I see their little faces twinkle as I enter the door each day. "How was your day, son?", I ask each of them. "Good, Daddy," they utter back with such confidence. What a precious way to end my day!

As a Christian man, father, husband, author and preacher of the Gospel of Jesus Christ, I am on a mission to

35

inspire, encourage, and challenge everyone within my sphere of influence. My mission in life is to reinforce why it is important to glorify God, the one who created us. God birthed us into this world for specific reasons: (a) to do His will and, at the same time, (b) to fulfill our purpose. Fatherhood falls in line with our purpose. Quite frankly, fatherhood, is in line with the purpose for all men, whether you actually father a child or not. Our lifestyles are the examples that the youth of this world observe to distinguish between right and wrong. Since they cannot see an invisible God, our role is to make God clear and visible through our lifestyles.

So far, we have learned that *father* is a noun, and derives from the Greek word *patēr,* meaning "a nourisher, protector, and upholder." This word, in its singular form, as written in *The Holy Bible*, is used 963 times! We have also learned that other forms of this word include:

- fathers – 522 times,
- father's - 146 times,
- fathers' – 10 times, and
- fatherless – 41times.

Further, there are 254 references to the Heavenly Father (*God Almighty*) throughout the Scriptures.

We also took a closer look at the biblical definition of what a father is: a *nourisher, a protector, and an upholder.*

A Nourisher

This means to supply with what is necessary for life, health and growth, to cherish or keep alive, and to strengthen or promote.

A Protector

This means to defend or guard from attack, invasion, loss, or insult, to cover, to shield, and to provide.

An Upholder

This means to support or defend, to lift upward, support, or raise, and to keep up or keep from sinking.

Abba is a biblical word for "'Daddy.'" It is an ancient Aramaic word and considered a peculiar term for Father-God, used by Jesus Himself. All three New Testament references are specific to God and shows that God is a loving, approachable Father:

a.   *"And He said, Abba, Father, all things are possible unto thee; take away this cup from me: nevertheless not what I will, but what thou wilt"* (Mark 14:36).

Here, Jesus addresses God with the household term for Father. This was unheard of in Palestinian Judaism at that time. It points to Jesus' unique relationship to God. So it is with the natural father. Because of the unique relationship that we have with the children that we have fathered, they should feel comfortable enough to approach us at any time, in any situation. Do you create an environment in which you children can approach you? Care for your children as God cares for us – His children.

b.   *"For ye have not received the spirit of bondage again to fear; but ye have received the Spirit of adoption whereby we cry, Abba, Father"* (Romans 8:15).

Abba becomes the intimate name that is only used by believers, in terms of our relationship with our Heavenly Father-God. The Holy Spirit places the believer as a son in God's family. *Abba* denotes the intimacy of the believer's relation to God. When our children call us "'Daddy,'" they are expressing a natural intimacy towards their natural father.

Biblically, there is no difference between the <u>love</u> that a father has towards his child, whether they become our children by natural birth or through adoption. We became children of God through the Spirit of adoption. Likewise, through the natural process of adoption, our children become ours. Either way, our ordained role as a father requires that we take proper stewardship over these precious little ones with unconditional love.

c.   *"And because ye are sons, God hath sent forth the Spirit of his Son into your hearts, crying, Abba, Father"* (Galatians 4:6).

Again, every child of God was divinely given the Holy Spirit the moment we were adopted by God. *Abba* represents the term by which the father was called in the affectionate intimacy of the family. The Spirit gives us an awareness that God is our Father.

The Word of God is consistent throughout *The Holy Bible*, from Genesis to Revelation. Fathers are called to *protect, nourish, and uphold.* When we fulfill this role, our children will indeed feel comfortable in our presence, know that they can approach us, will not be ashamed to cry on our shoulders, and will ask of us their hearts' desire, knowing that their father will respond with the truth. Be a father as God intended for you to be. God will surely smile upon you and the blessings upon your family will come through you as their conduit and as the head of your household. YOU ARE A FATHER. Love your ordained role and be fulfilled while doing it! What a precious word to hear: *Daddy.*

"Daddy" is such a precious word. When your child calls you "daddy," there is a tingle that sparks the fulfillment that it brings. Based upon what I have learned in this chapter, I will treasure the thought that my children are totally dependent upon me in the following ways:

1.
_____

2.
_____

3.
_____

4.
_____

5.
_____

... and I pledge NOT to let them down.

Chapter Five

Positive Effects of a Father's Presence

*"The father of the righteous shall greatly rejoice: and he that
begetteth a wise child shall have joy of him."*
(Proverbs 23:24)

*"Don't ever doubt the impact that fathers have on
children. Children with strongly committed fathers learn about
trust early on. They learn about trust with their hearts. They
learn they're wanted, that they have value, that they can afford
to be secure and confident and set their sights high. They get the
encouragement they need to keep going through the tough spots
in life. Boys learn from their fathers how to be fathers. I
learned all those things from my own father, and I count my
blessings."*
Former Vice President Al Gore, speaking at the National
Fatherhood Initiative's 3rd Annual National Summit on
Fatherhood in Washington, DC, June 2, 2000

As men, we must not waive nor forget our awesome

responsibility to our children, wives, and society at-large.

We are commanded by God's word to rule our homes well

(1 Timothy 3:4; 12). Upon returning from church services,

my family showered me with gifts and love on a recent

Father's Day Sunday. It was a carefully orchestrated demonstration of their love and appreciation to the man in their lives who is fulfilling his role as husband and father. It is a role that I choose to fulfill by the freewill granted unto me by my Heavenly Father (ABBA). My three boys made Father's Day cards at school and my wife went on a shopping spree at the neighborhood mall.

I often think about how it must feel to a child whose daddy has left home. His whereabouts are unknown. When the teacher says it is time to make Father's Day cards for the daddy's, what is a child to do when they know that they do not have a daddy? It must be very sad and lonely for that child. As already stated, fatherhood is a God-ordained role. We CANNOT fail. As father's, so much is dependent upon our presence, stewardship, involvement, and perseverance. God's word clearly and distinctly reveals that we are *nourishers, protectors, and upholders.* Further, documented evidence reveals the positive effects of a father's presence accordingly: [4]

- Studies link a sense of competence in daughters…to a close, warm relationship between father and daughter.
- Children whose fathers were highly involved in their schools were more likely to do well academically.
- A father's provision of warmth and control was positively related to higher academic achievement.

- The single most important childhood factor in developing empathy is paternal involvement.

- Children whose fathers were more involved in their care tended to have fewer teacher reports of negative "acting out" behavior.

- Boys whose fathers offered praise and compliments scored higher on tests of cognitive development.

- Children with "hands-on" fathers are much less likely to use drugs than children with "hands-off" or absent fathers.

- Men with greater marital satisfaction tend to be more involved with their children.

- Fathers who were able to provide economically for their children were more likely to be engaged with and nurturing of their children.

My reflections on Father's Day are noted below:

Father's Day reminds me of what is important in life
Each year, it brings me closer to my sons and my wife

It is a time of reflection, thought, and insight
And repeatedly instills in me a sense of what's right

To be a father is awesome and a privilege to share
All that I have, including possessions that my family will heir

I delight in the laws of God and to teach my sons the same
And to ensure their success, that is why Jesus came

Jesus Christ, the way, the truth, the life
Keeping that in mind as I show demonstrated love to my wife

During church services this day, we sat together and praised the Lord

As I observed the boys' reaction, I grow stronger all the more

As a father that stands tall and proud
I am unashamed to admit, that in my role, I feel as high as a cloud

So thank you, Jesus, for choosing me!
To be a loyal father and making me to be all that I can be

And thank you, God, for Jesus in whom I have life
For reminding me each of my responsibility to my love my wife

To all men who have failed to fulfill your role
Ask Jesus for forgiveness and he will restore your empty soul

For the remainder of this year and even way beyond
May all father's become real men and reestablish an everlasting bond.

"Daddy is my buddy."
Josh, age 10, as quoted by Mary Kay Stanley in *When I Think About My Father*

"Fathers' involvement has a unique impact on children's outcomes, including cognitive development, achievement, math and reading scores, as well as behavioral problems. The fact that this benefit is here should raise concern to those who do not have these resources."
W. Jean Yeung, Sociologist, University of Michigan, as quoted in Reuters Health News, June 12, 1999

I have learned from this chapter that in order to have a positive effect on my child's life, I will:

1. _____

2. _____

3. _____

4. _____

5. _____

Chapter Six

The Joys of Fatherhood

"...A wise son maketh a glad father: but a foolish son is the
heaviness of his mother."
(Proverbs 10:1)

What a joy to hear the words "'Daddy!'" each day when I arrive home from work. What a blessed privilege to know that my Heavenly Father entrusts me to raise three healthy sons in the midst of this dying world! What an honor to be a "'role model'" to young sons that will soon transition into young men. It is my behavior, lifestyle, mannerisms, and habits that they will emulate. It is my responsibility to train them in this present time in order that they clearly understand their God-ordained roles as husbands and

47

fathers in the very near future. What a joy, what a responsibility, what an honor!!

However, it begins before boys become men. This is evidenced in five powerful passages of Scripture, both Old and New Testament:

1.　*"Train up a child in the way he should go: and when he is old, he will not depart from it"* (Proverbs 22:6). Teach our children about the goodness and glory of God at an early age, so that, peradventure they stray away, they will know to call upon the name of Jesus in times of despair or trouble. The Word says, *"Neither is there salvation in any other: for there is none other name under heaven given among men, whereby we must be saved"* (Acts 4:12).

2.　*"(As it is written in the law of the Lord, EVERY MALE THAT OPENETH THE WOMB SHALL BE CALLED HOLY TO THE LORD)"* (Luke 2:23).

"Because all the firstborn are mine; for on the day that I smote all the firstborn in the land of Egypt I hallowed unto me all the firstborn of Israel, both man and beast: mine shall they be: I am the LORD" (Numbers 3:13).

"Sanctify unto me all the firstborn, whatsoever openeth the womb among the children of Israel, both of man and of beast: it is mine" (Exodus 13:2).

The Word teaches us that every male seed that is birthed into this world is called Holy unto Lord. As it pertains to the firstborn male, as was Jesus' birth (Luke 2:7), we belong to the Lord and are sanctified – set apart – for the Lord. What an impact we can have in this world if we teach our male children, at an early age, about what the Word says about them – AND LIVE IT!

3.   Luke 15:11-32 – In this *Parable of the Lost Son*, the obedience, lifestyle, mannerism, and dutifulness of the older son – the firstborn – was instrumental in assisting his father to win back his youngest son after a bout with riotous living.   The older son had recognized the importance of obedience and loyal service all of his life (verse 29). Unbeknownst to him, his younger brother had left home to experiment with unrighteousness.   When he realized that unrighteousness and sin was not fruitful, he asked to return home.   His father received him with open arms (verse 32), as a loving father should, and comforted his older son by saying, *"...for this thy brother was dead, and is alive again; and was lost, and is found."*

In this parable, this "certain" man is symbolic of the ordained position of fatherhood. Jesus teaches us through parables by using a natural example (a father with two sons – one obedient and one disobedient) to extract a spiritual meaning (the role of a Godly father).   Fatherhood is so vitally important to God's plan for redemption and salvation, as demonstrated by this "certain" man who showed compassion (verse 20) for his younger son knowing that he had strayed away from what he was taught. What is important is that he was lost and now he is found.

Jesus Himself expressed the same mandate in Luke 19:10 – *"For the Son of man is come to seek and to save that which was lost."* Still, he ordered the best robe and held a celebration at this return. The older son's impact on the life of his younger brother must be significant to his return. His example of obedience, loyalty and faithfulness became vivid in the mind of the younger brother when he fell to unrighteousness and felt its pain and discomfort. They both realized that what they learned at home, from their father, has more value than the destruction that the world has to offer.

The joys of fatherhood are never-ending and limitless! Since it is a God-ordained role and responsibility, true fulfillment is the end-result. The only two areas of my life that are more satisfying are my love for God – God *is* love - and my love for my wife. My challenge to all men is to get in line with God's plan for your life and learn the basics about fatherhood through His Word!

Clearly, the role of the father in the life of his children is critical to their overall well-being. Based upon what I have learned in this chapter, I commit to live in right-standing (righteousness) with God in the following ways:

1. _____

2. _____

3. _____

4. _____

5. _____

Chapter Seven

What is Righteousness?

"Blessed are they which do hunger and thirst after
righteousness: for they shall be filled."
(Matthew 5:6)

"But thou, O man of God, flee these things; and follow after
righteousness, godliness, faith, love, patience, meekness."
(1 Timothy 6:11)

Righteousness, the state of being in *"right*
standing" with God or uprightness before God, is
mentioned 304 times throughout the Old and New
Testaments of *The Holy Bible.* Other forms of this word,
righteousness' and righteousnesses, are used four and three
times, respectively. It is defined as *meeting the standards of*
what is right and just; morally right. Originating from the
Greek word *dikaiōma,* righteousness means holiness,
justice, and rectitude, and is an attribute of God only. The
righteousness of Christ includes His spotless holiness and

His perfect obedience to the law while on earth, and His suffering its penalty in our stead – *"For none of us liveth to himself, and no man dieth to himself"* (Romans 14:7). It is rightness by God's standards: *"Fear thou not; for I am with thee: be not dismayed; for I am thy God: I will strengthen thee; yea, I will help thee; yea, I will uphold thee with the right hand of my righteousness"* (Isaiah 41:10) and *"For he hath made him to be sin for us, who knew no sin; that we might be made the righteousness of God in him"* (2 Corinthians 5:21). It is also characterized by matching our life with God's commandments, love, and purposes, and it is action based upon love for God and a relationship with God.

Righteousness, like fatherhood, represents the state of doing what is right in the sight of God. Fatherhood, an ordained role of the male seed, is a precious and awesome responsibility. It is a role that must be taught, lived, and appreciated. This role brings total fulfillment if carried out according to God's purpose and His Word. There are seven "'kinds'" of righteousness as described in *The Holy Bible.* Men that desire a strong, intimate, loving, caring, and enduring fatherly relationship with their children, both sons and daughters, must pattern their actions after these seven 'kinds' of righteousness:

Created

Ephesians 4:24 – Recognize and acknowledge that God's plan for your life can, and will, be actualized

54

through Jesus Christ. Acceptance of Jesus Christ as your personal Lord and Savior symbolizes a "new birth." You have been salvaged – *made whole* – (mind, body and **spirit**). The REAL you must be born (again) and reconnected to your Heavenly Father (God), the One who created you. He will now begin to assemble in your life what is needed to carry out your pre-ordained role in this earth and disassemble those things that have, and will, hinder your growth and development in the Lord. *"…Put on the new man, which after God is created in righteousness and true holiness."*

Legal

Philippians 3:6 – To be right is to be obedient to God's law and His commandments. Staying in proper alignment with God allows Him to use you in a manner that will bring glory to His name. Do not rely upon your own strength but allow God to direct your paths concerning your role as a father.

Personal and Imputed

Philippians 3:9 – By faith, we are justified. By faith, we know that we can rely upon the Lord Almighty to help us to be the fathers that we are called to be. It is not through being self-righteousness, but *"through faith in Christ, the righteousness which is of God by faith."*

Experimental

Hebrews 5:13 – It takes time, work, patience, and experience to master the fulfilling role of fatherhood. Similarly, it takes time and much faith to develop an appreciation for righteousness. Experiences as a father and experiences with God will vary from person to person, but God wants and desires our righteousness so that He can use us to make Him clear and visible to a dying world. He also seeks strong fathers who will demonstrate to this world the importance of this ordained role and the family overall. Will you allow God to use you in this capacity?

Actual

Hebrews 11:33 – Hebrews, chapter 11, is often referred to as "The Hall of Faith." Old Testament saints are commended for their faith prior to Jesus. Through faith, they *"subdued kingdoms, wrought righteousness, obtained promises, stopped the mouths of lions...."* A desire to be in right standing with God is an attribute that has been sought since God inspired His prophets to record His Word through the Holy Spirit.

Real

1 John 2:29 – *"If ye know that He is righteous, ye know that every one that doeth righteousness is born of Him."* Knowing that Jesus Christ is the perfect example of righteousness, and we have His example in *The Holy Bible*, then fathers are without excuse to be examples to our children. To be right is not just an obligation because it is the right thing to do; it a divine responsibility that we inherited because we are Christian men. Christian men MUST be the standard of righteousness within the Body of Christ and the world at-large. To do so, study the Word of God and find all of the answers.

Based upon what I have learned in this chapter, I will live in right-standing with God because His Word teaches me to do so. Further, I will commit to a righteous lifestyle because:

1.

_____

2.

_____

3.

_____

4.

_____

5.

_____

Chapter Eight

Daniel, The Righteous Man

"But Daniel purposed in his heart that he would not defile himself with the portion of the king's meat, nor with the wine which he drank: therefore he requested of the prince of the eunuchs that he might not defile himself. Now God brought Daniel into favour and tender love with the prince of the eunuchs."
(Daniel 1:8-9)

Daniel is named amongst three men in *The Holy Bible*, by God Almighty, as righteous. Noah and Job are the other two (Ezekiel 14:14-20). His "right standing" with God kept him in proper position (alignment) to win the favor of God as well as change the lives of others within his sphere of influence. He was a governmental official and a prophet of God (Daniel 1:1-6 and Matthew 24:15). His gift of prophecy was evident early in life.

Daniel means *God is my judge*. While in exile, his name was changed to Belteshazzar, meaning *may he*

59

protect his life (Daniel 1:7 and 5:12), but this name did not stick with Daniel. Daniel's life was protected by God, not Bel. This young Jew was taken captive at an approximate age of 12 to 16, educated thoroughly (1:5), made a cupbearer, and trained for service in the Babylonian royal court. He firmly refused to do anything contrary to God's teachings, even when it meant risking his life. He kept the Jewish law of clean and unclean meat and was constant and faithful in his devotions to God.

Daniel wrote the *Book of Daniel* that shows, or demonstrates, God's guidance, intervention, and power in the affairs of men. As father's, men must be receptive and acknowledge that God leads, guides, and directs all of our actions, WHEN WE ALLOW HIM TO DO SO. Thus, the life of Daniel is a great example for men, in general, and fathers/husbands in particular, to emulate, follow, and study. The twelve chapters of this great book of *The Holy Bible* teach us that:

- **Daniel acknowledged his "'calling'" early in life.**

The gift of prophecy. His wisdom and divinely given interpretive abilities brought him into a position of prominence. He (and others) was chosen by the king of Babylon (Nebuchadnezzar) because he had the ability to stand in his palace and he was well taught (Daniel 1:4). Although this king intended to use Daniel's gift to serve an unknown god, he remained true to his love for God Almighty and refused to be changed because of his new surroundings. He chose not to be defiled by the king's practices, customs, food, and tricks. He knew not to serve any other gods!

- **Daniel is one of the few well-known Bible characters about whom nothing negative is ever written.**

This "greatly beloved" man of God (Daniel 9:23; 10:11, 19) was mentioned three times in the Book of Ezekiel as an example of righteousness. Righteousness (*dikaiosunē*) is defined in the original Greek translation as "the character or quality of being right or just." It was formerly spelled "rightwiseness." It is being in right standing with God, or positionally aligned. A man that is in the proper position with God is a man destined to fulfill his purpose in the earth and cause positive change around him.

- **Daniel's life was characterized by:**

    a. **Faith** – Daniel did not bow to the god of Nebuchadnezzar. He remained committed to God Almighty although he was threatened to change.

    b. **Prayer** – "*...he kneeled upon his knees three times a day, and prayed, and gave thanks before his God, as he did aforetime*" (6:10).

    c. **Courage** – "*Then Daniel went to his house, and made the thing known to Hananiah, Mishael, and Azariah, his companions: That they would desire mercies of the God of*

*heaven concerning this secret; that Daniel
and his fellows should not perish with the
rest of the wise men of Babylon"* (2:18-19).

d. **Consistency** – Daniel stood tall in the midst
of powerful kings, and did not move. He
was promoted as a reward.

e. **Lack of Compromise** – Daniel grew
stronger in the midst of trouble. He knew
that God was his protector.

▪ **Daniel repeatedly emphasized the sovereignty
and power of God over human affairs.**

Daniel was so unafraid of his circumstances,
punishment, and ridicule that he escaped unharmed from
the burning fiery furnace that was seven times hotter than
normal (3:19), as well as the lion's den in which the mouths
of the lions were shut. Daniel's love, respect, and honor for
God was so great that he also changed the hearts of two
kings because of his stance – Darius and Nebuchadnezzar.
Both kings attempted to change Daniel to serve their gods.
Instead, Daniel remained steadfast and caused *them* to
change to acknowledge the true and living God.

▪ **Daniel's pagan name – Belteshazzar - did not
"stick."**

King Nebuchadnezzar changed the names of Daniel and
the three Hebrew boys from Daniel, Hananiah, Mishael,
and Azariah, to Belteshazzar, Shadrach, Meshach, and
Abednego (1:7). However, we do not recognize Daniel's

pagan name because it did not last. For some reason, the other three pagan names of the Hebrew boys are, today, more popular than their original Godly names (1:6). During Sunday school lessons, students remember their pagan names with more frequency than they do their real names. Why? Because Daniel would not defile himself. Do not allow others to change your name to "Bubba," "Cool," or "Slick." Those type of names lead to destruction; They are not real! Take pride in who you are and what God has called you to do.

- **Daniel was granted wisdom and knowledge by God.**

"Then this Daniel was preferred above the presidents and princes, because an excellent spirit was in him; and the king thought to set him over the whole realm" (6:3).

- **Daniel took control of his environment and caused positive change.**

Through the life of this great prophet, we know that God can, and will, provide an escape route when we acknowledge Him and not the other gods of this world. The burning fiery furnace and the lion's den are constant reminders that God can get us out of any situation as long as we remain loyal and prayerful to Him.

A father – *a nourisher, protector and upholder* - is entrusted by God to be responsible for the lives in his household. This includes:

o **Financially** - Money for the home to meet the financial needs and paying the bills.

o **Materially** – Handling the material needs of the home including furnishing, cleaning, repairs, general maintenance, and upkeep.

o **Spiritually** – Praying for the home and family. Men are the conduit for the blessings of the family. You are the head, so take your rightful position.

o **Physically** – Being the example in your home of what it means to be physically fit and taking proper care of your *holy temple* (your body). Proper nutrition, health care, well-balanced meals, and drinking water in lieu of sodas.

o **Socially** – Initiating quality social time within the family structure. Family nights, family meetings, ensuring that everyone is at home for family meals, reading to the children each night, sharing homework responsibilities, and discussing your workday with your wife and children.

o **Professionally** – Adequate preparation for career progression. Developing a plan of action to perhaps double your multiple streams of income every five years through proper stewardship of your career and investments. This includes completing your education early in life, studying, being on time to work, doing your best while at work, learning about the financial markets as well as entrepreneurial opportunities, and seeking a mentor(s) to teach you how to progress in your chosen field of choice.

Playtime is over. Hanging out with the boys from the "'hood'" is over. Trying to be *cool* to impress others is over! God shows us, through His Word, how to live as Daniel and to be righteous men, fathers, and husbands. Learn from the life of this prophet of God. Study the chapters of this book. It will be an enriching, life-changing experience. Live it, learn from it, do it, be it, lead with it, share it, and profit from it. This country, more than anything else, needs Godly men to be the fathers that God has called us to be. It starts with one man at a time; let that man be YOU! Spend quality time with your F-A-M-I-L-Y. Remember, that means (F)ather (A)nd (M)other (I) (L)ove (Y)ou. Let your love extend to your FAMILY throughout this year and beyond.

Daniel's life exemplifies Godly character and conduct. He caused kings to change their thinking and their ways. Based upon what I have learned in this chapter, I will cause change within my sphere of influence in the following ways:

1.
_____

2.
_____

3.
_____

4.
_____

5.
_____

Chapter Nine
Acknowledge Your Calling

"Hear, ye children, the instruction of a father, and attend to
know understanding."
(Proverbs 4:1)

In an interesting report in the *U.S. News and World Report,* the number one priority, of the 50 mentioned, for the year 2005 stated: *Figure out what's important to you. The rest will follow.*[5] Under the headline is a photo of a dad and his four year-old son! If Dad is missing in action, not fulfilling his ordained role as Dad, and not being attentive to the needs of his children, he cannot give instruction. Much worse, the children do not get to know understanding without his instruction.

The United States headquarters of the National Fatherhood Initiative (NFI) is within 30 miles of my home in Maryland. Each year at their annual Fatherhood Awards Gala, NFI recognizes fathers who truly understand their important roles, at home and at work. During his speech at the 2004 gala, NFI President, Roland C. Warren, stated, "Through their roles as actors, business leaders, musicians, authors, and most importantly fathers, the individuals we are honoring this year have helped spread the message that involved, responsible, and committed fatherhood is an essential ingredient in building healthy children and a healthy society." As I read the "'who's who'" of award recipients each year, I could not help but wonder where they would be if *their* father's were missing. "Would they have fulfilled God's plan for their lives without their Dad?" I wondered. "Somehow, I think not."

One of the publications previously mentioned, from this phenomenal organization, *"Father Facts,"* is now in its fourth edition. This book is loaded with factual information concerning the essential role of the father. It is man's perspective but it confirms God's Word about the ordained role of the father – the head of the family. Here is some further vital information extracted from this book. The following key statistics can help us to better understand why there is so much dialogue going on about missing fathers:

1.   From 1960 to 1996, the number of children who lived in homes without a father or a stepfather rose steadily from 7 million to nearly 20 million. Since the mid-1990s, though, the number and proportion of children in father-

absent homes has leveled off. And the percentage of children living with both parents has remained fairly steady during the past decade.

2.   24 million children (34 percent) live absent their biological father.

3.   Nearly 20 million children (27 percent) live in single-parent homes.

4.   1.35 million births (33% or 1/3 of all births) in 2000 occurred out of wedlock.

5.   43 percent of first marriages dissolve within fifteen years; about 60 percent of divorcing couples have children; and approximately one million children each year experience the divorce of their parents.

(Unfortunately, this includes Christians!)

6.   Over 3.3 million children live with an unmarried parent and the parent's cohabiting partner. The number of cohabiting couples with children has nearly doubled since 1990, from 891,000 to 1.7 million today.

(Although adultery and fornication are sexual sins, this practice does not exclude Christians! Children mirror the behavior and lifestyle of their parents.)

7.   Fathers who live with their children are more likely to have a close, enduring relationship with their children than those who do not. The best predictor of father presence is marital status. Compared to children born within marriage, children born to cohabiting parents are three times as likely to experience father absence, and children born to unmarried, non-cohabiting parents are four times as likely to live in a father-absent home.

8.   About 40 percent of children in father-absent homes have not seen their father at all during the past year; 26 percent of absent fathers live in a different state than their children; and 50 percent of children living absent their father have never set foot in their father's home.

9.   Children who live absent their biological fathers are, on average, at least two to three times more likely to be poor, to use drugs, to experience educational, health, emotional and behavioral problems, to be victims of child abuse, and to engage in criminal behavior than their peers who live with their married, biological (or adoptive) parents.

(What a shame! The devastation to the children is generational. Where do you think that the term "Gen-X" derived? It is referring to a generation of children who grew up in unstable homes. One or both parents, specifically, Dad, was not in the home during the crucial years of development.)

10.   From 1960 to 1995, the proportion of children living in single-parent homes tripled, from 9 percent to 27 percent, and the proportion of children living with married parents declined. However, from 1995 to 2000, the proportion of children living in single-parent homes slightly declined, while the proportion of children living with two married parents remained stable.

11.   Children with involved, loving fathers are significantly more likely to do well in school, have healthy self-esteem, exhibit empathy and pro-social behavior, and avoid high-risk behaviors such as drug use, truancy, and criminal activity, compared to children who have uninvolved fathers.

(Why? Because Proverbs 22:6 says, "Train up a child in the way he should go: and when he is old, he will not depart from it.")

This morning, my middle son and I attended our monthly men's fellowship at our local church. During his exhortation, the teacher offered an expanded and more precise definition of a father. It was so revealing and gave me a different perspective on the awesome role of the father. First, he defined the family as follows: a group of people connected together by the same blood and functioning under <u>one head.</u> He taught us that a father:

(a) Protects the family from the spirit of death,

(b) Causes the family to become fully persuaded of the faithfulness of God,

(c) Seeks God's face on behalf of the family,

(d) Makes the power of God visible by conforming to His moral character,

(e) Is to remain in a state of righteousness, and

(f) Is to remain in a state of prayer.[6]

The father is the foundation of the family. The foundation is defined as the base upon which something rests. If Dad is missing, what about the family unit, structure, existence, and well being?

The facts speak for themselves. Fathers should take the lead in providing for our children. Our presence alone makes a tremendous difference and positive impact. Based upon what I have learned in this chapter, I will raise my children to become the Godly men and women in the following ways:

1.
_____

2.
_____

3.
_____

4.
_____

5.
_____

Chapter Ten

Consequences of Father Absence for Children

"One father is more than a hundred school masters."
17th century English proverb

Chief among threats to this generation of children, particularly boys, is the breakdown of the family. Every other difficulty we will consider has been caused by or is related to that fundamental tragedy. It can hardly be overstated. Stable, lifelong marriages provide the foundation for social order. Everything of value rests on those underpinnings. Historically, when the family begins to unravel in a given culture, everything from the effectiveness of government to the general welfare of the people is adversely affected. This is precisely what is happening to us today. The family is buffeted and undermined by the forces operating around it. Alcoholism, pornography, gambling, infidelity, and other virulent infections have seeped into its bloodstream.[7]

Your foundation is your family. The person who does not builds up their home, the same has torn it down.[8] Father's Day is always celebrated on the third Sunday in the month of June. It symbolizes a day set-aside to recognize and acknowledge the role of fathers. To highlight the critical importance of the role of the father, this chapter exposes the <u>consequences of father absence for children.</u>[9]

If the father is missing in action, not fulfilling his ordained role as Dad, and not being attentive to the needs of his children, he cannot give instruction. Much worse, the children do not get to know understanding without his instruction. Choices are long lasting and life changing! When men make the choice to abandon our children, we cannot choose the devastating consequences. The consequences of our absence in the home has a direct and negative impact on our children through the following means: child abuse, crime, drug and alcohol abuse, education, emotional and behavioral problems, physical health, poverty, and sexual activity. Let's explore each of these eight areas.

Child Abuse

The overall rate of child abuse and neglect in single-parent households is 27.3 children per 1,000, whereas the rate of overall maltreatment in two-parent households is 15.5 per 1,000.

Crime

> *"Boys need same-sex role models to define themselves as male. When fathers are absent, young males are more likely to exaggerate their purported masculinity."*
> Kathleen Heide, Ph.D., Professor of Criminology,
> University of South Florida, 1997.

In a longitudinal study of 6,403 males who were 14 to 22 years old, it was found that after controlling for family background variables such as the mother's education level, race, family income, and number of siblings, as well as neighborhood variables such an unemployment rates and median income, boys who grew up outside of intact marriages were, on average, more than twice as likely as other boys to end up in jail.

Drug and Alcohol Abuse

Fatherless children are at a dramatically greater risk of drug and alcohol abuse. No matter what their gender, age, family income, and race/ethnicity, adolescents not living with both parents (biological or adoptive) are 50 to 150% more likely to use substances, to be dependent on substances, and to need illicit drug abuse treatment than adolescents living with two biological or adoptive parents.

Educational Challenges

"If America's Dads got as involved as America's Moms in their children's education, America's children would be studying harder and getting a lot more A's. Dads make a powerful difference in defining expectations and challenging children to do their best."

Former U.S. Secretary of Education

Richard W. Riley, 1997.

Based on a study of 17,110 children, researchers found that a child who did not live with both parents was 45% to 90% more likely to have been the subject of a parent-teacher conference than a child who lived with both biological parents.

Emotional and Behavioral Problems

"'Father hunger' often afflicts boys ages one and two whose fathers are suddenly and permanently absent. Sleep disturbances, such as trouble falling asleep, nightmares, and night terrors frequently begin within one to three months after the father leaves home."

Alfred Messer, *"Boys' Father Hunger: The Missing Father Syndrome,"*

Medical Aspects of Human Sexuality 23, January 1989.

Children in single-parent families are two to three times as likely as children in two-parent families to have emotional and behavioral problems.

Physical Health Challenges

> *"Some of our nation's most urgent problems, ranging from infant mortality, to drug abuse, to AIDS, to teen pregnancy, to the disproportionately poor health and excess mortality afflicting the children of our minority citizens...arise precisely from an erosion of basic values, and the collapse of the institutions that teach them, like family and community."*
> Former Department of Health and Human Services
> Secretary Louis W. Sullivan, 1991.

Poverty

Children in father-absent homes are five times more likely to be poor. Nearly 75% of American children growing up in single-parent families experience poverty for some period during their first 10 years, compared to 20% of children in two-parent families. More than 75% of all unmarried teen mothers go on welfare within five years of the birth of their first child.

Illicit Sexual Activity

> *"Today with the rise in illegitimacy and divorce, fewer fathers are around to protect and defend their daughters' safety and honor. With more girls lacking the love and attention that only a father can give, more of them are willing to settle for perverse alternatives, namely, seeking intimacy with predatory adult men."* Gracie S. Hsu, *"Leaving the Vulnerable Open to Abuse,"*

Perspective, September 9, 1996.

The above statistics should serve as a wake-up call. To be honored by loved ones on this special day, Father's Day, is humbling and moving. It shows that we are loved, needed, and appreciated. However, when we look at the state of our society, much work needs to be done to improve the overall conditions around us. We can start in *our homes, with our children.* These statistics and facts should motivate us to continue to be Godly fathers. If you have fallen short in your responsibility and accountability, now that you know better, DO BETTER. Do you part to save the next generation.

*Sources:
1. www.morning-glow.com
2. *Father Facts*, 4th Edition, Wade F. Horn, Ph.D. and Tom Sylvester, National Fatherhood Initiative © 2002
3. www.crcw.princeton,edu
4. www.childtrends.org

Parental absenteeism is detrimental to the well-being of our children. Based upon what I have learned in this chapter, I will consciously be engaged with my children most frequently by:

1.
_____

2.
_____

3.
_____

4.
_____

5.
_____

Chapter Eleven

Save the Seed

"And, ye fathers, Provoke not your children to wrath; but bring them up in the nurture and admonition of the Lord."
(Ephesians 6:4)

Prisons are populated primarily by men who were abandoned or rejected by their fathers. Of the thousands interviewed, not one of them genuinely loved his dad. Ninety-five percent of those on death row hated their fathers. In 1998, there were 1,202,107 people in federal or state prisons. Of that number, 94 percent were males. Of the 3,452 prisoners awaiting execution, only forty-eight were women. That amounts to 98.6 percent males. Clearly, it is far easier to build strong children than to repair broken men [10].

One Sunday in the recent past, the Washington, DC metropolitan area endured its second significant snowstorm of this young winter season. Thus, my family and I were not able to attend worship service at our local church as we are accustomed. Taking the lead as the family man that God has called me to be, I led worship service in my home with my wife and three young sons. My sons opened service in prayer, my wife read a scripture, I led praise and worship as we sang together, and I delivered the sermon. We had a great time together – as a *family!* I recognize and acknowledge that I am the natural example in my home. My children will know God because of me. I have determined that I will not consider my responsibility as some small task but to see it as a major undertaking that is worthy of top priority!

I thank God for my former pastor. It was over 10 years ago, on May 2, 1993, that his sermon entitled *"The State of the Local Church"* captured my attention, arrested my conscience, and caused my wife and I to run to the altar to confess Jesus Christ as our personal Lord and Savior. It was the first Sunday of the month that we accepted Christ, partook in Holy Communion, and joined the church. The church was fifteen minutes from our home and I remember that day as if it just recently happened. Not long ago, after six years in New Jersey, we relocated back home to Maryland so that we could again be a part of the marvelous things happening in that local church in Temple Hills.

During his 22 years as pastor, he has taught a message entitled *"Save the Seed."* [11] This is the second time that he has taught from this thought-provoking and life-changing message. My passion for men to become good fathers and husbands goes beyond one particular man or one particular home; it has to do with the next generation of men. Raising today's boys into tomorrow's men is what is at stake.

In a society that is rapidly deteriorating and becoming more tolerant of anti-social behavior, it is critical that the father in *each* home raise his boys to be Godly men. Our society, and world at-large, depends on this. That is why, in this chapter, we should focus on Ephesians 6:4 ...*"bring them up in the nurture and admonition of the Lord."* The word "'nurture'" is used only once in *The Holy Bible* and the word "'admonition'" is used three times, all in the New Testament. The Random House Webster's College dictionary defines nurture and admonition as follows:

1.   **Nurture** – To feed and protect, to support and encourage, and to bring up, train, and educate.

2.   **Admonition** – Counsel, advise, and a gentle reproof.

In the Greek, "'nurture'" is synonymous with "'chastening'" *(paideuō)*, which denotes "to train children," suggesting the broad idea of *education.* Notice that whenever God instructs, through His Word, about the role of the father, it leads back to the biblical definition of a

85

father *patēr,* meaning *"a nourisher, protector, and upholder"*.

As I study the vast resources, statistics, and information that are available concerning the topic of "fatherhood," it saddens me to think of the millions of boys whose dads did not nourish, protect, or uphold them. The statistics are astonishing. I study from 18 major sources, including the United States Department of Health and Human Services/Fatherhood Initiative, The Brookings Institution, Child Trends, The National Fatherhood Initiative, National Center for Children in Poverty, United States Census Bureau, and The Heritage Foundation, just to name a few. However, my most relevant study comes from the Word of God, as He confirms over and over and over again the devastation to society of the absentee father.

We "'save the seed'" by teaching, exposing, and training our boys, at an early age, about the glory of God. We save them from the wiles of the devil by equipping them with Godly principles from an early age, by teaching them how to pray and how to be Godly fathers and husbands throughout their young lives. We are to be their natural example as Jesus Himself is our natural example. In doing so, on a consistent basis, we then make God – our Heavenly Father – clear and visible to the next generation. Our impact now will produce ethical government leaders, good pastors with effective sermons that change lives as God intended, outstanding community leaders that raise the level of awareness in their neighborhoods, senior executives in the workplace with character and morals, tenderhearted brothers, and excellent fathers in each home. Join me in saving the seed...

God's Word teaches us to educate our children and give them good counsel in accordance with the Scriptures. Based upon what I have learned in this chapter, I will raise my children in the nurture and admonition of the Lord in the following ways:

1.

_____

2.

_____

3.

_____

4.

_____

5.

_____

Chapter Twelve

Why Are Men Under Attack?

"...The thief cometh not, but for to steal, and to kill, and to destroy..."
(John 10:10)

Another year is upon us. It is a time for new beginnings for us all. When it was only eleven days into another new year, I wondered to myself, "Where are the men?" This question transcends racial barriers. Is there a deliberate scheme, plan, or game that is designed to alter the truth? Can our men really know and understand who they are and act out of character with such regularity, with no remorse, without conscience, and unaware of the consequences? What's preventing God's Word from penetrating into them to cause positive change? Why aren't they running to the altar to ask Jesus into their lives?

What's happening and why is it happening? Why are our men under attack?

The answer is clear. Yes, *we* are under attack. Unfortunately, they are working to the detriment of our women, children and communities. Statistics clearly reveal the following facts:

- Every year, more boys are born than girls.
- By the third grade, our boys demonstrate a lack of interest in school.
- Throughout the criminal justice system, our men are incarcerated with more frequency than women.
- More men are addicted to drugs, alcohol, illicit sex (it is reported that men and boys spend, on average, 11 hours per week on the internet viewing pornography), and tobacco than women.
- Men have a shorter life span than women.
- Men are less prepared to attend college than women. College campuses hold at least three times the number of women than men.
- Men are less likely to read books than women. Eighty percent of the buyers of books are women.

There are three primary ways that Satan attacks us:

- Intellectual defilement is designed to cause us to delight in things that exalt themselves against the knowledge of God. Our minds are the divine center of "choice." We can make choices because we have a free will. However, we cannot choose the consequences. If we make choices outside of the will of God, the consequences are often catastrophic.

- Spiritual defilement is designed to cause us focus on the *natural* versus the *spiritual* things of this world. In the original Greek translation, natural things are defined as *pragma* whereas the spiritual things are defined as *rhema* (spoken word), and *logos* (place or territory).

- Physical defilement includes:
  - **Smoking** – Inhaling foreign substances into our bodies (holy temples). This primarily involves abusing plants that God intended for purposes other than ingestion for perverted pleasure.
  - **Food** – The initials for the Standard American Diet are S-A-D. The American diet is sad in that it a primary reason why 70% of Americans are overweight. It often begins in children and manifests itself into adulthood. This leads to chronic ailments in the body that rob us of long life, energy, the ability to get a good night's sleep, and good blood circulation. African-American men in particular, suffer from high blood pressure and diabetes at alarmingly high rates – more than any other group of men on the planet.

o **Drugs** – All "drugs" come from the plants that God caused to grow. They are abused and misused and have become the object of our desire. Cocaine, PCP, crack, and marijuana come from plants. Instead of us taking dominion over them, as instructed in Genesis 1:26, they are laughing at us! The plants are actually controlling us, including our love of money, also made from a plant.

o **Illicit Sex** – This begins with lust and ends in disaster. It saddens me to think of all of the broken homes, relationships, and families as a result of a man's three minutes of pleasure with a woman that he was not married to. Need I say more?

Through these methods of attack, our adversary, the devil, seeks to confuse us and keep us from knowing the following five key points concerning the man's role as husband and father:

▪ **The head of the wife is the husband** (Ephesians 5:23).

God is a God of order. Just as Jesus Christ is the head of the church (Ephesians 5:23), the husband is the head in his home and is to raise his children in the nurture and admonition of the Lord (Ephesians 6:4).

- **The family is the foundation of the church, the community, and the society.**

- **Satan does not want man to know his created role.**
  When we understand our role, we become the natural example in our homes. We live, serve, teach, lead, protect, comfort, pray, encourage, and motivate, just as our Heavenly Father does for us – his children.

  - **Every male should cause his house to follow him into the Kingdom of God.**
    The Kingdom of God is His system, the system that we operate in as new citizens (Colossians 1:13). However, men are logical thinkers – we are left-brained. One of the most effective ways to get more men into the body of Christ is for them to see other men's lifestyles mirror the teachings of Jesus. To see us praise Him, pay tithes and offerings with a cheerful heart, pray, sing songs, openly weep, and not be ashamed of the gospel. Most of our churches are filled each week with women. They can access both sides of the brain. As men hear more challenging sermons, see more Godly men in action, and understand the love of God, they are more likely to take their rightful roles as Godly men.

    - **The lifestyle of every male seed should uphold the integrity of God.**
      We are ambassadors for Christ (2 Corinthians 5:20), thus, we represent Him in the earth. We must become the substance of things hoped for, the evidence of things not seen. Allow God to be glorified through our lives so that

others will desire to have a personal relationship with Him. That only comes through Jesus Christ.

Until we enter into a relationship with God, through Jesus Christ, *The Holy Bible* teaches us that we are lost, helpless, alienated, and shut off from God. We are subject to the power of darkness (Satan) and defenseless (cannot help ourselves) in this world.

As men make a renewed commitment to better understand our roles as husbands and fathers, always remember that our children need us. The fear of the Lord is the beginning of knowledge (Proverbs 1:7). Our thirst for Godly knowledge will teach us to be led, guided and directed by the Word of God. He is our source. Our *Abba* Father loves us and cares for us (John 17).

As a man of God, I will protect and cover myself, and my family, through the Word of God daily. Through prayer and supplication, meditation, activities, and my thoughts, I will encourage myself to fight off the obstacles in this world that come against my God-ordained position as father and husband. Based upon what I have learned in this chapter, I will do so in the following ways:

1. _____

2. _____

3. _____

4. _____

5. _____

Chapter Thirteen

Family Time and Family/Work Conflict

"I think quality time is just a way of deluding ourselves into shortchanging our children. Children need vast amounts of parental time and attention. It's an illusion to think they're going to be on your timetable, and that you can say 'O.K. we've got half an hour, let's get on with it.'"
- Dr. Ronald Levant, as cited by Laura Shapiro, "The Myth of Quality Time," *Newsweek, May 12, 1997.*

"Parents are too busy spending their most precious capital – their time and their energy – struggling to keep up with MasterCard payments... They work long hours to barely keep up, and when they get home at the end of the day they're tired."
- Harvard Psychiatrist Robert Coles, 1991.

"*"The Joys of Fatherhood'"* is a series of articles, written from my heart, designed to foster change in the hearts of men and women that read them on a regular basis. With a specific focus on "*fatherhood,'"* God has given me a platform to encourage ALL adults to recognize the importance of our parental responsibilities and priorities. If

I were to ask you, "What is more important, your job or your children?," the majority of you would say, "My children." Now, observe your daily routine as you juggle job, church, recreational, parental, leisure, and personal responsibilities.

I ask you again, "What is more important, your job or your children?" If you are honest and evaluate how you spend your time, you will answer, "My job." The amount of time and energy that it takes to prepare for work, commute to and from work in today's traffic, and wind down once you arrive at home, surpasses the amount of time that you spend with your children. The impact is more devastating than we may think or know!

What we consider important in life dictates how we prioritize of lives. In his book, *Managing Time*[12], we should carefully consider our priorities as follows:

God	Work
Family	Relationships

Facts concerning attitudes about **Family Time and Father Time** [13]

- In a telephone survey of 200 12- to 15-year-olds and 200 parents, 21% of the children reported their top concern was not having enough time with their parents, whereas only 8% of parents said their top concern was not having enough time with their children. This survey was conducted in 1999.

- Fathers with high levels of participation in childcare have higher self-esteem and feel more competent and satisfied in their parental role.
- Business management tends to view work/family balance as a "woman's issue."
- Teens with parents who are in the home are less likely to try alcohol, tobacco, or marijuana.
- Fathers' share of childcare more that doubled between 1965 and 1998.
- On average, a child in a two-parent family spends 1.2 hours each weekday and 3.3 hours on a weekend day directly interacting with his or her father. Overall, the average total time fathers in two-parent families are engaged with or accessible to their children is 2.5 hours on weekdays and 6.3 hours on weekend days.
- Percent of children reporting a close relationship with their father, by family type:
  o Married – 51%
  o Divorced/Separated – 30.1%
  o Never married – 20%

Facts concerning attitudes about family/work conflict and stress:

- A MasterCard survey found that close to 85% of fathers polled said "the most priceless gift of all" was time spent with family.

- In a national survey of 2000 adults, 55% agreed that "Employers giving parents more flexible work schedules so they can spend more time with their children" was a "'very effective'" way of helping children.

- When 1,500 Chief Executive Officers and human resource directors were asked how much leave is reasonable for a father to take after the birth of a child, 63% indicated "none."

- 72% of men and 83% of women reported they experienced "a lot" of work/family conflict, up from just 16% in 1992.

- National polling data reveals that in 1999, 58% of Americans believed employers do not recognize the strain fathers face when trying to balance the demands of family and the demands of work, up from 28% in 1996.

- Father with more flexible work schedules report less role strain and lower levels of marital, professional, and parental stress.

While it will always be a challenge to spend as much time as we would like with our children, Jesus teaches us to walk as children of *light* and to redeem our precious time (Ephesians 5:16) in the midst of these evil days. To redeem our time means to carefully evaluate how we spent each and every minute. Fathers, make it a priority to spend time with your children outside of working hours by:

    a) Assisting them with their homework.

    b) Volunteering to coach little league baseball or basketball.

    c) Going on roller skating outings.

    d) Taking them bowling.

    e) Teaching them how to ride a bicycle.

    f) Playing Scrabble or other game boards.

All of the above are valuable and joyful ways to spend quality time with family. Get to know your children and have them get to know you! After all, they are God's gift to you. Take proper stewardship of your gift…

I will shift my priorities from "how to make a living" to "how to live" in accordance with the Word of God. The choice to spend more quality time with my family is mine. I choose it now. Based upon what I have learned in this chapter, spending more time with my family will result in:

1. _____

2. _____

3. _____

4. _____

5. _____

FATHERS: TEST YOURSELF

The family at peace regularly:

- Guards against weeds of bitterness and unforgiveness.
- Takes care of little issues before they become big problems.
- Makes regular deposits in every family member with affirmations.
- Gives the children a chance to teach and be taught. [14]

Understanding the responsibility and stewardship involved with fatherhood, I am determined to be an excellent example in the earth for my children. Based upon what I have learned in Part I: The Significance and Role of a Father, I will serve them and help them to avoid the following negative incidences:

1. _____

2. _____

3. _____

4. _____

5. _____

Part II.

The Impact and Role of a Mother

"Who can find a virtuous woman? for her price is far above rubies. The heart of her husband doth safely trust in her, so that he shall have no need of spoil. She will do him good and not evil all the days of her life."

(Proverbs 31: 10-12)

Resourceful

Loving

Compassionate

Endearing

Strong in the Lord

Respects Her Husband

Nurtures Her Children

A Good Friend

Her Husband's Glory

Wise

Life Giver

Trustworthy

Blessed

Similar to the establishment of a Father's Day celebration, man also established a special day to acknowledge and recognize the "role" of motherhood. This day, of all days, our *mothers* are to be celebrated. Here is the story of Mother's Day:

The earliest Mother's Day celebrations can be traced back to the spring celebrations of ancient Greece in honor of Rhea, the Mother of the Gods. During the 1600's, England celebrated a day called *"Mothering Sunday."* Celebrated on the fourth Sunday of Lent (the 40 day period leading up to Easter), *"Mothering Sunday"* honored the mothers of England.

During this time many of the England's poor worked as servants for the wealthy. As most jobs were located far from their homes, the servants would live at the houses of their employers. On Mothering Sunday the servants would have the day off and were encouraged to return home and spend the day with their mothers. A special cake, called the *mothering cake*, was often brought along to provide a festive touch.

As Christianity spread throughout Europe the celebration changed to honor the *"Mother Church"* - the spiritual power that gave them life and protected them from harm. Over time the church festival blended with the Mothering Sunday celebration. People began honoring their mothers as well as the church.

In the United States Mother's Day was first suggested in 1872 by *Julia Ward Howe* (who wrote the words to the Battle hymn of the Republic) as a day dedicated to peace. Ms. Howe would hold organized Mother's Day meetings in Boston, Massachusetts every year.

In 1907 *Ana Jarvis*, from Philadelphia, began a campaign to establish a national Mother's Day. Ms. Jarvis persuaded her mother's church in Grafton, West Virginia to celebrate Mother's Day on the second anniversary of her mother's death, the second Sunday of May. By the next year Mother's Day was also celebrated in Philadelphia.

Ms. Jarvis and her supporters began to write to ministers, businessmen, and politicians in their quest to establish a national Mother's Day. It was successful in that by 1911 Mother's Day was celebrated in almost every state. President Woodrow Wilson, in 1914, made the official announcement proclaiming Mother's Day a national holiday that was to be held each year on the second Sunday of May.

While many countries of the world celebrate their own Mother's Day at different times throughout the year, there are some countries, such as Denmark, Finland, Italy, Turkey, Australia, and Belgium, which also celebrate Mother's Day on the second Sunday of May.

The impact and role of the mother is so significant, thought-provoking, and meaningful to God, that He references "*mother,* " and its variations, in *The Holy Bible,* 325 times:

> ➤ Mother – 244 times,
>
> ➤ Mother's – 73 times,
>
> ➤ Mothers – 7 times, and
>
> ➤ Mothers' – once.

Further, *The Holy Bible* is much more descriptive of a godly woman in the book of Proverbs 31:10 - 31 than it is relative to a godly man and children. This concentrated passage of Scripture describe, in detail, the godly attributes of a wise woman as being happy, resourceful, strong, busy, influential, and endearing.

Chapter Fourteen

To God be the Glory!

"...but the woman is the glory of the man. For the man is not of the woman; but the woman of the man. Neither was the man created for the woman; but the woman for the man."
(1 Corinthians 11: 7-9)

For starters, **Glory** represents and reflects a *divine* quality. It literally reveals the brightness, splendor, and radiance of God's presence. It is God's revelation of Himself. Our word "'doxology'" comes from "'*doxa*,'" the Greek word for glory. It is a word that is referenced 394 times in *The Holy Bible*. Many different variations of this word includes:

- ➢ Gloriest
- ➢ Glorieth
- ➢ Glorified
- ➢ Glorifieth

111

➢ Glorifying

➢ Glorious

➢ Gloriously

The Wife is to be Honored

The Book of First Peter teaches how, and why, to have character and conduct above reproach. Having been born again to a living hope, we are to imitate the Holy One who has called us. The fruit of this our character will be conduct rooted in submission, wives to husbands, husbands to wives, and Christians to one another.

Submission in marriage is not one way. Rather, it is to be a shared experience as an expression of love to one another. Chapter 3 begins with instruction to the wife relative to her husband. This preceded similar instruction concerning submission to government and submission in business. Again, our Heavenly Father is teaching us about character and conduct as Christians. Then, there is specific instruction to husbands to honor their wives.

"Likewise, ye husbands, dwell with them according to knowledge, giving honour unto the wife, as unto the weaker vessel, and as being heirs together of the grace of life; that your prayers be not hindered."
(1 Peter 3:7)

Honor is due her, as the Word states, so that the husband's prayers are not hindered and that there will be recognition that the two are heirs together. Such honor is welcomed, expected, and due to the wife.

112

Love Your Wife as Yourself

The Book of Ephesians emphasizes two main points throughout its six chapters:

➤ The Position of the Christian (what)

➤ The Practice of the Christian (how)

In chapter 5, Paul strongly encourages the saints at Ephesus to know the value of family and the relationship that it requires to flourish. Beginning in verse 22, he challenges the wives to submit to their husbands, the husbands to love their wives, and in chapter 6, for the children to obey their parents. Verse 25 of chapter 5 is the operative verse in that husbands are encouraged to *"...love your wives even as Christ also loved the church, and gave Himself for it."* In verse 33, he writes *" ...let every one of you in particular so love his wife even as himself..."*

"FOR THIS CAUSE SHALL A MAN LEAVE HIS FATHER AND MOTHER, AND SHALL BE JOINED UNTO HIS WIFE. AND THE TWO SHALL BE ONE FLESH. This is a great mystery: but I speak concerning Christ and the church. Nevertheless let every one of you in particular so love his wife even as himself; and the wife see that she reverence her husband."
(Ephesians 5:31-33)

God *is* love (1 John 4:8). As an expression of a man's love for his wife, he makes God clear and visible, thus, easy to follow. More so, when a man demonstrates that he loves who he is, the wife and children naturally follow. For this reason, the husband is the head of the wife (Ephesians

5:22). As a man follows Christ, the wife follows and respects him.

Be Affectionate

First Corinthians, chapter 7 provides a detailed roadmap for the principles of married life, principles for the unmarried, and principles for remarriage. This book of *The Holy Bible* is written to a corrupt church and addresses a variety of problems in the lifestyle of this church, including factions, lawsuits, immorality, questionable practices, and spiritual gifts. Then, in the midst of the book, Paul instructs this church on the principles of married life.

Affection is a deserved attribute that husbands must demonstrate to their wives. It symbolizes a caring, compassionate, and loving emotion that wives crave. It is an expression of love, trust, and warmth. It is even a means to communicate "I Love You" without actually uttering the words. The wife expects it and the husband is responsible to deliver it.

"Let the husband render unto the wife due benevolence: and likewise also the wife unto the husband. The wife hath not power of her own body, but the husband: and likewise also the husband hath not power of his own body, but the wife."
(1 Corinthians 7:3-4)

Husbands are extremely proud of their wives. God's Word describes the wife as the man's GLORY. Based upon what I have learned in this chapter, I will do the following to ensure that my GLORY is forever acknowledged by me, as the husband:

1.

_____

2.

_____

3.

_____

4.

_____

5.

_____

Chapter Fifteen

An Help Meet

*"And the LORD God said, It is not good that the man should be
alone: I will make him an help meet for him."*
(Genesis 2:18)

God created the woman to be a response
mechanism. As a woman, and a mother in particular, you
are designed to *respond* to a need. A woman is also fit,
adaptable, and flexible. Thus, the *help meet* description of a
woman (Genesis 2:18) characterizes her as fit and
adaptable for man and for her role/purpose in the earth.

Genesis 2:18-25 fills in the details of the simple
statement in Genesis 1:27, ...*"male and female created He
them."* This account particularly amplifies the "and
female" part of the statement and shows how woman was

created. Three observations can be made from this passage of Scripture that will help us to understand how the family began:

The Need for Woman

Women are absolutely essential to God's plan. It was God who observed, *"It is not good* that the man should be alone (verse 18)," and determined to make a *"help meet"* for Adam. Woman's role in the will of God is/was to be a "help" who is/was suitable to man in every particular mental, spiritual, emotional, social, and physical need. God undertook an orientation program to show man the need that He alone had observed. He brought to man the birds and beasts He had created, so that man should exercise his dominion over them (verse 28) and name them (verse 19). However, in verse 20, it is noted that for Adam there was no "help" similar to him alone.

The Provision of Woman for Man

In verses 12-24, God caused man to go to sleep, and He removed one of his "ribs." Exactly what God removed is not known, but it was adequate for His purpose. He "made" (built) a woman (verse 22) who Adam recognized as being his equal, "bone of my bones, and flesh of my flesh." This resulted in what has become known as the universal law of marriage (verse 24), in which it can be seen that:

(1)   The responsibility for marriage is on the man's shoulders. He is to "leave his father and mother."

(2)   The responsibility for keeping the union together is on the man's shoulders. He is to cleave unto (stick to) his wife.

(3)   The union is indissoluble. God's Word says "they shall be one flesh."

The State of the First Man and Woman

Verse 25 teaches us that from the beginning, the man and woman were "naked" in each other's presence and "were not ashamed." There is no shame in nudity when it occurs within the right context – the marital union. This passage clearly teaches that (1) Sex was God's idea and is not sinful, (2) sex came before the Fall, and if the Fall had never taken place there still would be sexual relations between a man and his wife, and (3) propagation of the species is one, but not the exclusive, purpose for sex.[15]

In the Book of Deuteronomy, Chapter 6, a new generation of Israel is gathered on the plains of Moab to hear Moses review the Law in preparation for their entrance to the Promised Land. The previous generation had died in unbelief in the wilderness. Moses begins his instruction by telling the people of Israel what a home is all about. He sets forth three components that must be true if the home is rightly related to God:

There must be a Revelation of God

God revealed three things about Himself in verse 4: (1) His eternality (LORD; Hebrew *Yahweh*, The Eternal), (2) His plurality (*Elohim*, Hebrew plural of God; there are three Persons in the Godhead), and (3) His unity – "one LORD" – the three Persons of the Godhead constitute one God. Each is essential.

There must be a Response to God's Revelation

The response is to be a total response of love with all one's being - heart, soul, and mind - as revealed in verse 5. This is the only fitting response to the eternal God who has revealed Himself.

There must be a Threefold Responsibility

In verses 6 through 9, this responsibility acts as a check upon the proper response. If the earthly father, through the help of a mother/wife, responds to God with love, he will be fulfilling his threefold responsibility. It is: (1) To have God's truth govern his heart (verse 6), (2) To have God's truth govern his home as evidenced by the father teaching truths of God's revelation to his children by both formal (teach diligently) and informal (talk of them) instruction, and (3) To have God's truth govern his habits and conduct personally, privately, and publicly. In short, the home is to be a divine school in which the father, with the *help* of the mother, is to be the teacher, under Christ.[16]

As an outer expression for the love that I have for my husband, and based upon what I have learned in the chapter, I will do the following to "help" him to achieve (meet) the desires of his heart as well as God's plan for his life:

1.

_____

2.

_____

3.

_____

4.

_____

5.

_____

Chapter Sixteen

A Life Giver

"Every good gift and every perfect gift is from above, and cometh down from the Father of lights, with whom there is no variableness, neither shadow of turning."
(James 1:17)

A genuine faith will produce real changes in a person's conduct and character, and absence of change is a symptom of a dead faith.

A mother, who gives life to a child, presents the possibility of that child knowing Jesus Christ as Saviour. In the Book of James, chapter 1, verse 17, three great principles are presented:

(1) God is the Father, or Creator, of the heavenly bodies.

(2) As their Creator, He is certainly more stable than they. With God, there is not even the slightest change, for He is immutable.

(3) God is only good.

In this context, the mother can be viewed as the conduit for the child to come into the knowledge of God the Father, the Creator, and the One who is good.

Eve, whose name means *life*, is the mother for all of mankind. She was the first created woman, created secondarily from Adam (or man) as a helpmeet for him, and later named, and designated, as the mother of the human race. Two names were given to her, both bestowed by man, her mate. The first is derived from the Hebrew word, *ishshāh*, for woman, and literally means "man-ess." This is not strictly a name, but a generic designation that refers to her relation to the man. This represents a relation in which she was created to fulfill in default of any true companionship between man and beasts, and represented as intimate and sacred beyond that between parents and their children (Genesis 2:18 – 24).

The second, Eve, or "life," given after the transgression and its prophesied results, refers to her function and destiny in the spiritual history or evolution of which she is the beginning (Genesis 3:16:20).

In both instances, one fact remains quite clear. God created the woman as His way to give life to the seed of man. She literally gives life in her biological role that results in a life-long maternal role. As the giver of life, a woman, and a mother in particular, brings life to her family in every situation, circumstance, test, trial, and temptation in a number of ways, including:

Gives birth

...the vessel, used by God, to birth new life into the earth.

Gives nourishment

...nourishes the child during development in the womb and after birth into the earth. Her nourishment protects the child from harm, hurt, and disease.

Encourager

...encourages her husband and children to dream big and actively pursue life's goals.

Soft spoken

...is non-threatening in her approach to give counsel, advice, and feedback to her family. It is a welcomed deviation from the harsh criticism that the worldly system offers all too often.

Motivator

...motivation is the catalyst needed to complete a task. This needed boost of confidence, that a mother can provide, is key to the family's structure, unity and stability.

Inspirer

...inspires her family to greatness by improving

weakenesses and rewarding strengths.

Consoler

...understands the power of consoling versus criticizing, especially with young children.

Reinforcer

...rewards family members, especially children, for a job well done.

Optimist

...sees the glass as half full in lieu of half empty. She chooses not to worry excessively.

Supporter

...supports her family in all facets of life.

Helper

...assists her husband and children to fulfill their Godly purpose in the earth.

Lover

...demonstrates a genuine, unconditional love for her family. This love generates a warm feeling of comfort and protection.

The valuable gift from God as a life-giver, dates back to His original intent for the woman (James 1:17). Cherish the gift, receive it, value it, accept it, and most importantly, walk in it!

I give LIFE to situations, circumstances, and ideas. As a vessel of God, I intend to give LIFE, based upon what I have learned in this chapter, in the following ways:

1.

_____

2.

_____

3.

_____

4.

_____

5.

_____

Chapter Seventeen

A Type of Christ

Then Jesus said unto them, *"Verily, verily, I say unto you, Moses gave you not that bread from heaven; but my Father giveth you the true bread from heaven. For the bread of God is He which cometh down from heaven, and giveth life unto the world."*
(John 6:32-33)

A woman (wife) is a type of Christ in that she will give her life to deliver a child. She is sacrificing her lifestyle, daily routine, and life to carry a child for nine months without charge. The child then lives to make an impact in the earth because it is born with purpose while in the mother's womb (Jeremiah 1: 5).

In the Book of John, chapter 6, verses 31 through 35, Jesus describes Himself to his disciples in Capernaum as *"...the bread of life."* In other words, this means the

129

bread that gives life. The life of which He speaks is *spiritual and eternal.* Jesus goes on to teach *"...he that cometh to me shall never hunger; and he that believeth on me shall never thirst."* The type of Christ that a woman symbolizes is one who gives life *naturally.* In this regard, she sacrifices, from conception to birth – a nine-month process – and even as the child grows, matures, develops, and enters into adulthood – from a newborn through college age and beyond, to ensure that a child has a healthy and productive natural life. This child is ensured, based upon the mother's love for it, meals so that it will not go hungry, and drink to avoid dehydration.

What happens during Pregnancy?

Giving birth is indeed a sacrifice. As a result of the fall of man in the Garden of Eden, God pronounced *"...I will greatly multiply thy sorrow and thy conception; in sorrow thou shalt bring forth children..."* (Genesis 3:16). Pregnancy is a three-phase process, divided into trimesters. Women are encouraged to draft a birth plan to minimize the nine-month sacrifice that lies ahead. An article extracted from the Childbirth.org website is found below as an example to follow:

A Birth Plan
By: Robin Elise Weiss, LCCE[17]

Birth plans are ideas and expectations that you have about the birth of your baby. They are used to help people, who come into contact with you during your labor and birth, know a bit more about you, how you have prepared for this baby, and what you want from the birth.

A lot of people misunderstand and assume that you are writing orders for people to follow. Ah, if only labor would allow us to do this.

Most people have preferences for how things are to be done during the labor and birth. A birth plan might address some of the following issues:

- Do you want mobility or do you wish to be confined to a bed?
- Do you want a routine IV, a heparin/saline lock, or nothing at all?
- Do you want to wear your own clothing?
- Listen to music?
- Use the tub or shower?
- Do you want pain medications or do you want to avoid them?
- Do you have preferences for which pain medications you want?
- Would you prefer a certain position in which to give birth?

- Would you like an episiotomy? Or, are there certain measures you want used to avoid one?
- If you need a cesarean, do you have any special requests?
- For home and birth center births, what are your plans in case of transport?

The First Trimester

Changes in Your Body

During the first three months of pregnancy, or the first trimester, your body is undergoing many changes. As your body adjusts to the growing baby, you may have nausea, fatigue, backaches, mood swings, and stress. Just remember that these things are normal during pregnancy, as your body changes. Most of these discomforts will go away as your pregnancy progresses. And some women might not have any discomforts! If you have been pregnant before, you might feel differently with this pregnancy. Just as each woman is different, so is each pregnancy. And, as your body changes, you might need to make changes to your normal, everyday routine. Here are some of the most common changes or symptoms you might experience in your first trimester:

- Tiredness,
- Nausea and vomiting,
- Dizziness,
- Constipation,

- Leg cramps,
- Varicose veins, and
- Nosebleed and bleeding gums.

The Second Trimester

Most women find the second trimester of pregnancy to be easier than the first trimester, but it is important to stay informed about your pregnancy in this stage too. While you might notice that symptoms like nausea and fatigue are going away, you will see other new, more noticeable changes to your body. Your abdomen will expand as you gain weight and the baby continues to grow. And before this trimester is over, you will feel your baby beginning to move! Many of the other symptoms you had in the first trimester might also continue, like constipation or leg cramps, so it is important to keep doing all of the healthy things you have already learned to help prevent or treat those symptoms. Here are some things you might experience during this trimester:

- Aches and Pains,
- Shortness of breath,
- Stretch marks, and
- Tingling and itching.

The Third Trimester

You could still be having some of the same discomforts you had in your second trimester, but now you will notice that you may have to go to the bathroom more often or that you find it even harder to breathe. This is because the baby is getting bigger and it is putting more pressure on your organs. Don't worry, your baby is fine and these problems will lessen once you give birth. You also might have some of these changes:

- Heartburn,
- Swelling,
- Hemorrhoids, and
- Tender Breasts.[18]

The Woman as a *Type* of Christ

The Holy Bible lists twenty-two different titles of Christ. The most popular two are **Jesus**, a transliteration of the Hebrew word *Joshua*, which means "Yahweh is Salvation," and **Christ**, a translation of the Greek term *Christos*, meaning "Anointed One" or "Messiah." Below are selected names of Christ in terms of how He sacrificed His life to redeem us spiritually, as compared to selected names for mothers and how they sacrifice their lives to birth us naturally.

TABLE 1:

Name or Title of Christ	Significance of Christ	Biblical Reference	Significance of a Mother
Chief Cornerstone	A sure foundation for life	Ephesians 2:20	A sure foundation for the rest of our lives, beyond childhood
Chief Shepherd	Protector, sustainer, and guide	1 Peter 5:4	Protector, leader
Emmanuel (God with us)	Stands with us in all of life's circumstances	Matthew 1:23	Always there and accountable for our well-being
Good Shepherd	Provider and caretaker	John 10:11	Keeper of the home
Great Shepherd of the Sheep	Trustworthy guide and protector	Hebrews 13:20	Leads, guides and directs in the natural
Lamb of God	Give His life as a sacrifice on our behalf	John 1:29	Gives her life as a sacrifice to birth us into this world
Light of the World	Brings hope in the midst of darkness	John 9:5	Brings hope during troubled times
Mediator between God and men	Brings us into God's presence redeemed and forgiven	1 Timothy 2:5	Mediator between father and children
Son of man	Identifies with us in our humanity	Matthew 18:11	Identifies with us as her child
The Word	Present with God at the creation	John 1:1	Present with us at conception in her womb

I acknowledge my role as a type of Christ. As I lay down my life for the sake of my children, and based upon what I have learned in this chapter, I will continue to fulfill my role in the following ways:

1.

_____

2.

_____

3.

_____

4.

_____

5.

_____

Chapter Eighteen

Keeper of the Home

"But speak thou the things which become sound doctrine: That the aged men be sober, grave, temperate, sound in faith, in charity, in patience. The aged women likewise, that they be in behaviour as becometh holiness, not false accusers, not given much to wine, teachers of good things; That they may teach the young women to be sober, to love their husbands, to love their children."
(Titus 2:1-4)

God has ordained that man be the custodian over the family (1 Corinthians 11:3), however, the wife has stewardship of the home.

One of the two major points in the Book of Titus is to set things in order. God is a God of order (1 Corinthians 14:40). Good works are desirable and profitable for all believers, but everything has an order. The Apostle Paul writes a comforting message to a young pastor, Titus, encouraging him to appoint men and woman of proven spiritual character in their homes and businesses, and to oversee the work of the church. The bottom-line is that men and women, young and old, each has vital functions to fill in the home and church if they are to be living examples of the doctrine they profess. In this passage of Scripture, beginning in chapter 2, the older women are taught to instruct the younger women about holiness, to love their husbands, and to love their children. As the husband fulfills his ordained role, as the head, the rest of the family naturally follows. The wife now makes God clear and visible through her husband's example and, in turn, assists her husband by making God clear and visible to the children in the home.

In this text, domestic regulations are clearly taught. Spiritual character is a key theme throughout. The aged men, as referenced in Titus 2:1, are elderly men. They are to be sober (sensible), grave (dignified), temperate (prudent and thoughtful, sound (healthy) in faith, in charity (love), and in patience. Thus, these aged men are to be examples of godliness to the younger men. The aged women, older women, are to be in behavior (demeanor) as becometh holiness. They must thus be teachers of good things by teaching the young women to be sober, to love their husbands, and to love their children. The older women are to teach the younger by their example. Discreet means modest and decent. Chaste is sexually pure. Keepers at home means workers at home, no idle. Obedient to their husbands means being submissive to their *own* husbands.

As the keeper of my home, and based upon what I have learned in this chapter, I will maintain my home in the following ways:

1.

_____

2.

_____

3.

_____

4.

_____

5.

_____

Chapter Nineteen

Characteristics of the Godly Woman

"Strength and honour are her clothing; and she shall rejoice in time to come."
(Proverbs 31: 25)

Do women have a role in the society today? How about the church, on the job, and in the home? You bet they do. From a biblical perspective, that is a very silly question. The scriptures – God's Word - undeniably and unquestionably verify that women *do* have a place as well as an active role in society, on the job, in the church and in the home. Their roles are dynamic, insightful, and worthy of further examination. On a personal note, my covering was at one time provided out of love by a woman pastor whom I respect and honor.

Women are represented in all walks of life today, being used as a willing vessel by God, to fulfill the position of homemaker, employee, mentor, counselor, pastor (leader and shepherd), elder (overseer), deaconess (servant), evangelist (one who proclaims the gospel through the Holy Spirit), and prophetess. It is recorded throughout *The Holy Bible* about the importance of the role of women, and their character, especially as it relates to salvation and redemption. Jesus Christ, God's only begotten Son, teaches us valuable lessons about why and how He related to women during His three and one-half year earthly ministry. To this end, a look at the lives and historical impact of five women, and their godly character, is worthy of mention.

In the original Greek language, "'the church'" is derived from the word *ekklesia* (*ek* – "out of", and *klēsis* – "a calling"). It was used among the Greeks as a body of citizens "gathered" or "assembled" to discuss the affairs of state. Its meaning is to congregate, thus, the gatherers at any given public worship service are commonly referred to as the "congregation." It, too, is derived from the Greek word *ekklēsia*. The church *is* you and I. We comprise the church and we are taught in Hebrews 10:25, "*Not forsaking the assembling of ourselves together, as the manner of some is; but exhorting one another: and so much the more, as ye see the day approaching.*" Why? To encourage one another, love one another, and hear what God has to say to

142

us through His Word (*rhema*). Outside of the "church," people (men, women, and children) congregate where we meet: Restaurants, jobs, school, homeowners association meetings, bus stops, train stations, and airports.

To understand the impact and significance of how God relates to people, let's observe two important passages of Scripture that will settle our hearts and minds. First, God is no respecter of persons (Romans 2:11), that is, He does not distinguish between male and female when He is searching for a willing vessel to get His will done in the earth. Instead, He requires a *clean* vessel – one who does not willingly or consistently commit sin against Him - with an open heart toward Him. God is interested in our clean hands and pure hearts, not our gender.

> *"Then Peter opened his mouth, and said, Of a truth I perceive that God is no respecter of persons."*
> (Acts 10:34)

Second, God's Word establishes its accuracy, inerrancy, and everlasting truth by repeating itself through the writings of many different authors. His Word says, *"It is written in your law, that the testimony of two men is true."* (John 8:17)

Let's examine the lives of five women mentioned in *The Holy Bible* and how they were used by God to fulfill His plan to redeem and salvage (save) man after the sin of Adam in the Garden of Eden. Notice the characteristics of these women that made them useful for the Master's plan.

143

These women are Mary (Jesus' mother), the Samaritan woman, Rahab the harlot, Mary Magdalene, and Phoebe, a deaconess.

Mary (Jesus' mother) – Jesus, the Son of God, is God's plan to redeem mankind back to Him. Thus, Jesus had to be born of man (Son of man), that is Mary, in order to fulfill this plan. Mary was entrusted by God to carry Jesus for nine months in the womb, as conceived by the Holy Spirit. She was espoused (not yet married) to Joseph at the time of conception. Mary and Joseph cooperated with this plan of God so that the Old Testament scripture would be fulfilled.

"BEHOLD, A VIRGIN SHALL BE WITH CHILD, AND SHALL BRING FORTH A SON, AND THEY SHALL CALL HIS NAME EMMANUEL, which being interpreted is, God with us." (Matthew 2:23)

Mary was a young Jewish girl engaged to the carpenter Joseph when God revealed to her that she was to be the mother of the Messiah. Joseph, advised of these events in a dream and knowing Mary was miraculously pregnant, took Mary as his wife. Toward the end of her pregnancy, the couple from Nazareth traveled to Bethlehem for a taxation census, and Jesus was born there. Mary was present at Jesus' crucifixion and became one of His followers after His resurrection.

She was instructed to call his name Jesus.

She did. Mary exemplifies the spiritual principle of OBEDIENCE. Through obedience, Mary is a demonstration of how one person can be used by God to change mankind forever. Because of Jesus, we are saved!

The Samaritan Woman – In the book of John, chapter 4, Jesus reveals Himself to an unnamed woman that He ministered to in Samaria even before He revealed Himself unto His handpicked disciples (John 4:26). Samaritans were a race of persons formed when Jews married non-Jews. Jews intensely hated Samaritans and often refused to set foot in Samaritan territory. Jesus demonstrated that God loves Samaritans, just as God loves Jews.

On Jesus' journey through Samaria, He stopped at Jacob's well and asked "a woman of Samaria," *"Give me a drink"* (John 4:7). His disciples had gone away to buy food during this exchange. This woman's curiosity piqued as she wondered why a Jew would engage in conversation with her. It is commonly known that the Jews had no dealings with the Samaritans (verse 9). Jesus began to teach a valuable lesson at the well to this woman: The water in the well will quench one's current thirst, but they will thirst again. However, the free gift of God is LIVING WATER and is symbolic of everlasting life (verse 14). When this woman answered Jesus' question honestly concerning her promiscuity, He knew that the time was right to reveal Himself to her.

This Samaritan woman exemplifies HUMILITY and TRUSTWORTHINESS. God trusted her and revealed Himself to her before He revealed Himself to His own handpicked disciples (all men).

Rahab, the Harlot – The name means "violence"; "pride, arrogance," yet Rahab's name is specifically mentioned in the genealogy of Jesus Christ (Matthew 1:5). The great, great grandmother of King David, Rahab is included amongst the faithful in Hebrews, chapter 11. She was a prostitute from Jericho who hid two Hebrew spies and provided escape for them (Joshua 2:1). Later she and her family were spared when the city was destroyed. Rahab was the mother of Boaz.

Rahab's hope and faith in her knowledge of God's plan for escape prompted her to act on what she believed (Joshua 2:10-17). Rahab exemplifies FAITHFULNESS.

Mary Magdalene – She was healed by Jesus and became one of His closest followers. She was present at Jesus' crucifixion and a witness of His resurrection. As a resident of the city of Magdala, she was one of the women who came to the tomb to anoint Jesus and discovered that He had risen. Mary of Magdalene's name is specifically mentioned in the Scriptures – the first of two - amongst the women who ministered to Christ.

"And it came to pass afterward, that he went throughout every city and village, preaching and shewing the glad tidings of the kingdom of God: and the twelve were with him, and certain women, which had been healed of evil spirits and infirmities, Mary called Magdalene, out of whom went seven devils."
(Luke 8:1-2)

This Mary was further instructed by Jesus, at His appearance to her after the resurrection, to *"go tell my brethren that they go into Galilee, and there shall they see me"* (Matthew 28:10). Mary Magdalene exemplifies COMPASSION and CARING. Her compassion moved to action was a comfort to Jesus and acknowledged by Him when he asked her to deliver a message to the brothers of Galilee. He knew that she could be trusted.

Phoebe – In chapter 16 of the Book of Romans, the Apostle Paul is praising and thanking multiple women (and men to a lesser degree) for their diligent work in the church at Rome. In verses 1 and 2 in particular, Paul recognizes and acknowledges the work of a deaconess named Phoebe as follows: *"I commend unto you Phoebe our sister, which is a servant of the church which is at Cenchrea. That ye receive her in the Lord, as becometh saints, and that ye assist her in whatsoever business she hath need of you: for she hath been a succourer of many, and of myself also."* She is mentioned first amongst all that are mentioned in the entire 16th chapter. Notice also that her role in the church is specifically mentioned as if to distinguish her, and her diligent works, from the others.

Phoebe exemplifies LOYALTY and DILIGENT SERVICE. Phoebe's excellent work in the ministry was worthy of mention to one of the greatest men in biblical times. Not all women who did similar work were mentioned by name.

What is the role of the woman in society today and what constitutes Godly character? It is the same for all who have confessed Jesus Christ as their personal Lord and Saviour, and are children of the Most High God:

> ➢ Love God,
> ➢ Hate sin,
> ➢ Give of self (*as a servant*),
> ➢ Live holy,
> ➢ Represent God in the earth (*through a Godly lifestyle*),
> ➢ Draw others to Christ,
> ➢ Lift up the name of Jesus through every word, thought and deed,
> ➢ Obey the Scriptures, and
> ➢ Exemplify excellence in ministry.

God has demonstrated repeatedly, through His Word, that He uses women mightily to accomplish His will in the earth. I will therefore pattern my life after the Godly women in this chapter to effect positive change in the world. I will do the following:

1. _____

2. _____

3. _____

4. _____

5. _____

Understanding the responsibility and stewardship involved with motherhood, I am determined to be an excellent example in the earth for my husband and my children. Based upon what I have learned in Part II: The Impact and Role of a Mother, I will serve them and help them to avoid the following negative incidences:

1. _____

2. _____

3. _____

4. _____

5. _____

Part III.

The Phases and Role of the Child

"My son, hear the instruction of thy father, and forsake not the law of thy mother: For they shall be an ornament of grace unto thy head, and chains about thy neck."

(Proverbs 1:8)

"Hear, ye children, the instruction of a father, and attend to know understanding."

(Proverbs 4:1)

Learner

Dependent

Inquisitive

Innocent

Naïve

Trusting

Reliant

Eager for Attention

Happy

Loving

Follower

Observant

An Heritage

The central reason for marriage is to provide children with mothers and fathers in a safe and loving environment.[19] That said, children have two primary responsibilities in life: Obey their parents *in the Lord* while they are young, and honor and cherish their parents later in life, for the remainder of their lives.

Simply put, children are a gift from God! The references in *The Holy Bible* to child(ren) are close to 2,000 times as follows:

> ➤ Child – 198 times,
> ➤ Child's – 4 times,
> ➤ Children – 1,735 times,
> ➤ Children's – 18 times, and
> ➤ Childhood – twice.

Both the Old and New Testaments agree that children have only one responsibility in the family – to obey their parents. The admonition of Solomon is more fully explained by the Apostle Paul in the Book of Ephesians 6:1-3: *"Children, obey your parents in the Lord, for this is right. Honour thy father and mother; which is the first commandment with promise; That it may be well with thee, and thou mayest live long on the earth." Children* is an inclusive term. It is not a matter of either sex or age that is involved.

Twice in Scripture God has intervened and directly stated what He would have children do. The last time was nearly 2,000 years ago when He gave a revelation to Paul

153

for the church. The first time was nearly 3,400 years ago when He gave a revelation to Moses and Israel in which He commanded, *"Honour thy father and thy mother."*

God's will for children is that they obey their parents. Two things are promised to children who obey their parents: It will be well with them (they will have a happy life), and they will have a long life. These are the two things that children want most, and obedience to parents is the only way to assume them. That is why this is the first commandment with promise; from it springs all of the other important issues of life. The child who has not learned to obey his parents, who are God's representatives in the family, will not learn to obey God.

Chapter Twenty

Children Are God's Heritage

"Lo, children are an heritage of the LORD: and the fruit of the womb is his reward."
(Psalm 127:3)

Authority is God's plan to protect our lives.[20] Our children are ultimately under our authority while being raised. In essence, they are under our protection since they cannot fend for themselves prior to adulthood. Marriage is the means by which the human race is propagated, and the means by which spiritual teaching is passed down through the generations.[21] It, too, is covered under the spiritual principle of authority as God's way to protect the sanctity of the family.

155

In this context, the five verses in Psalm 27 are quite endearing passages of Scripture. Three of the five verses reference God's unconditional love specifically to children:

An Heritage

In verse 3, "*...children are an heritage of the LORD.*" This literal translation means "the status gained a person through birth."[22] We remind our children daily that God is the Heavenly Father by making Him clear and visible through lives and lifestyle.

Strong and Mighty

In verse 4, "*As arrows are in the hand of a mighty man; so are children of the youth.*" When this Scripture is cross-referenced with Psalm 112:2, the literal translation means that the seed of a righteous man shall be mighty upon earth, representing a generation of the upright that shall be blessed. The clearer our roles become within the family unit, the clearer the child can understand what it means to be a Godly child: Obedient and honorable to their parents.

Plentiful

In verse 5, God is communicating to us what an honor it is to be entrusted with stewardship of His children! As fathers and mothers of multiple children, we will be happy, we will not be ashamed, and we will be defended in a time of need.

Children, and parents, have a joint responsibility to be mindful that God created all things (Psalm 24:1). We were created for His pleasure. His Word comforts us each day in that, *"Blessed is every one that feareth the LORD; that walketh in His ways* (Psalm 128:1). *"*

Children are an heritage of the Lord. Based upon what I have learned in this chapter, I will uphold and love my children in the following ways:

1.

_____

2.

_____

3.

_____

4.

_____

5.

_____

Chapter Twenty-One

Obedience At All Costs

"My son, keep thy father's commandment, and forsake not the law of thy mother: Bind them continually upon thine heart, and tie them about thy neck. When thou goest, it shall keep thee; and when sleepest, it shall keep thee; and when thou awakest, it shall talk with thee. For the commandment is a lamp; and the law is light; and reproofs of instruction are the way of life."
(Proverbs 6:20-23)

Obedience is God's plan to reward our lives.[23] It is up to us to teach our children that God holds the parents responsible and accountable for them.

Obey has two meanings in its original Greek form:

a.   *hupakoē* (noun) – "Obedience and/or of the fulfillment of God's claims or commands."

b.   *Hupakouō* (verb) – "To listen, to attend." "To submit, to obey."

It is a profound word that is found 69 times in *The Holy Bible* and other variations of the word obey include obeyed, obeyedst, obeyeth, and obeying. Some of the key passages in the Old and New Testament that teach children, and parents, about this spiritual principle include:

Obedience to Parents is Well Pleasing Unto the Lord

> *"Children, obey your parents in all things: for this is well pleasing unto the Lord."*
> (Colossians 3:20)

Obedience demonstrates an ability to follow instruction and to be teachable. It is commonly mentioned in church circles that God loves **F-A-T** people:

F   aithful

       A   vailable

              T   eachable

This principle should begin at an early age and become habit-forming. During adulthood, we will have fewer challenges with surrendering to authority and obedience will become a part of our lives. Since parents are entrusted by God to have wise stewardship over their children, it is well pleasing unto the Lord when they listen, follow, obey, and benefit. That is God's plan.

Deuteronomy 6:5 - 7 has an excellent teaching on this principle, "...*thou shalt love the LORD thy God will all thine heart, and with all thy soul, and with all thy might..."""...And thou shalt teach them diligently unto thy children..."*

When thou sittest in thine house...

Spend quality time together at the breakfast or dinner table, watching television, during family meetings, playing board games, or chatting on the couch. Just be sure to communicate, constantly, about the goodness of God in their lives.

When thou walketh by the way...

Walking to the pool in the summer-time or walking to the gym during the winter months, let your child know that God is good all the time. God made the sun for warmth, the rain for the vegetation that He causes to grow, and the snow to beautify the earth. Make sure that your child knows that and rejoices in it.

When thou lieth down...

Prior to bedtime, say prayers together.

When thou riseth up...

Allow your children to see you first as they rise for another day that the Lord has made. Rejoice in it together!

Correction as Needed

"...and reproofs of instruction are the way of life
(Proverbs 6:23)."

A sign of love is for the parents to correct the child. Correction sometimes comes in the form of a good spanking.

"He that spareth his rod hateth his son: but he that loveth him chasteneth him betimes"
(Proverbs 13:24).

Correction begins at an early age...When you are older, you will remember not to repeat past mistakes. It may hurt now, but you will appreciate it later in life.

"Chasten thy son while there is hope, and let not thy soul spare for his crying"
(Proverbs 19:18).

Correction is intended keep off of the path of destruction. You are programmed to want to do wrong. If allowed to do what you want, you are destined for destruction and heartache.

"Foolishness is bound in the heart of a child; but the rod of correction shall drive it far from him"
(Proverbs 22:15).

The sting of the correction is short-term. What you learn from the correction is long-term.

"Withhold not correction from the child: for if thou beatest him with the rod, he shall not die"
(Proverbs 23:13).

God commands the parent(s) to correct the children that they are entrusted with to train, lead, guide, and direct. This is part of the training, formal and informal, that leads to a productive and Godly life.

"The rod and reproof give wisdom: but a child left to himself bringeth his mother to shame. When the wicked are multiplied, transgression increaseth: but the righteous shall see their fall. Correct thy son, and he shall give thee rest; yea, he shall give delight unto thy soul"

(Proverbs 29:15-17).

Hearken unto the advice and counsel of your mother and father. It is a wise thing to do.

"My son, hear the instruction of thy father, and forsake not the law of thy mother"
(Proverbs 1:8).

Honor your father and mother...

"Hearken unto thy father that begat thee, and despise not thy mother when she is old"
(Proverbs 23:22).

...If you do not honor them, you cannot fulfill your purpose in the earth. God's plan for your life will be cut off.

"And he that smiteth his father, or his mother, shall be surely put to death. And he that stealeth a man, and selleth him, or if he be found in his hand, he shall surely be put to death. And he that curseth his father, or his mother, shall surely be put to death"
(Exodus 21:15-17).

A life in keeping with God's design and instruction brings the greatest possible fulfillment, while any deviation from His design invites disaster. The Scripture teaches that true freedom and genuine fulfillment can be found only when we live in harmony with our design.[24]

Children are commanded by God to obey their
parents. Based upon what I have learned in this
chapter, I will encourage my children to obey me (us)
through my (our) Godly example(s) in the following
ways:

1.

_____

2.

_____

3.

_____

4.

_____

5.

_____

Chapter Twenty-Two

Growth and Development of the Child

"Train up a child in the way he should go: and when he is old, he will not depart from it."

(Proverbs 22:6)

Proverbs 22:6 is a biblical prescription for rearing children. This verse reveals two key ingredients in the prescription: First, the command, *"Train up a child in the way he should go,"* and second, the promise, *"when he is old, he will not depart from it."* The command involves three parts:

The Concept of Training: "Train Up"

This does not denote corporal punishment but rather includes three ideas:

(1) **Dedication** – This is the consistent meaning of the word in its other Old Testament occurrences

    i.   Deuteronomy 20:5

    ii.   1 Kings 8:63

    iii.   2 Chronicles 7:5

Child training must begin with dedication of the child to God. Parents must realize that the child belongs exclusively to God and is given to the parent only as a stewardship.

(2) **Instruction** – This is the meaning of this word as it is used in the Jewish writings. The parents are to instruct or cause their children to learn everything essential in pleasing God.

(3) **Motivation** – This is the meaning of this word in Arabic, as it is used to describe the action of a midwife who stimulates the palate of the newborn babe so it will take nourishment. Parents are to create a taste or desire within the child so that he is internally motivated, rather than externally compelled, to do what God wants him to do.

The Recipient of Training: "A Child"

This is one of the seven Hebrew words translated by the English word *child* and would better be translated by our word *dependent*. As long as the child is dependent on

166

his parents, he is to be the recipient of training, regardless of his age.

The Content of The Training: "In The Way That He Should Go"

The thought is that at each stage of his development the parents or guardians are to dedicate, instruct, and motivate the child to do what God evidently has best equipped the child to do for Him. This is graphically illustrated by Joshua when he said, *"but as for me and my house, we will serve the LORD"* (Joshua 24:15).

If the command has been kept, the promise can be claimed. The promise includes the certainty of realization – *"he will not depart from it."* If the commandment has not been kept, the promise will not be realized. Rearing children is not an overnight occurrence; it takes careful forethought and conscious obedience on the parts of the parents.[25]

The Life of Jesus As A model

The growth, development, maturation and ultimate fulfillment of Jesus' life is worthy of examination. In this society, unfortunately, it has been determined that a child is legally "ready" and responsible to handle the following activities at a predetermined age:

TABLE 2:

Activity	Age Limit	Outcome
Drink alcohol	21 years	Drunkenness, dependency, irresponsibility
Drive a car	16 years, 9 months	Non-owner breeds unappreciation for usage of parent's car
Have sex	Generally starts at 14 years	Unprepared for the unexpected outcomes, such as pregnancy, sexually-transmitted diseases, guilt, attachment (love), and abandonment (often by boys toward girls)
Earn wages from a job	14 years	An understanding of financial stewardship
Cell phone usage	Generally starts as early as 11 years	Inability to manage calling plan and lack of steady funds to pay overage fees
Partying	Freshman in high school, or 14 years	Loud music leads to violence and ultimately leads to illicit sex
Bypass educational opportunities as presented	Graduation from high school (or before), or 17 years	The beginning of shattered dreams, hopes, and life-long aspirations

The Book of Luke interprets the life of Jesus in a manner worthy of emulating in today's society. The life of Jesus, both as the son of man and the son of God, is a testimony in and of itself. He lived in the earth for 33 ½ years and was on a specific assignment from His Father – to save and redeem mankind. Observe what He accomplished! His first twelve years was spent in training. Luke 2:42 reveals that Jesus, a Jewish male, became a full member of the religious community at age 13. By age 12, He underwent preparation for this. *"And when He was twelve years old, they went up to Jerusalem after the custom of the feast."* After twelve years of their annual feast of the Passover in Jerusalem, Jesus stayed behind, without His parents' knowledge (Luke 2:45). Following a three-day search for Him, his parents found Him in the temple, amongst the teachers and asking questions (2:46). Amazed at what their son had learned within twelve years, Jesus responds to his parents' inquiry, thinking that He was lost, *"How it is that ye sought me? Wist ye not that I must be about my Father's business"?* (2:49). Jesus' reply was indicative of His readiness to begin training for His purpose on earth – *To seek and to save that which was lost"* (Luke 19:10). For 18 years, he prepared to enter into His divine purpose. He was baptized by John (3:21), empowered by the Holy Spirit to carry out His purpose (3:22), and received His official confirmation from our Heavenly Father to enter into His purpose through these words: *"Thou art my beloved Son; in thee I am well pleased"* (3:22).

Then, *The Holy Bible* reveals that Jesus was 30 years old when He began His three-and-a-half year ministry by teaching, training, and encouraging His hand-picked disciples about how to carry out the Great Commission: *"Go ye therefore, and teach all nations, baptizing them in the name of the Father, and of the Son, and of the Holy Ghost; Teaching them to observe all things whatsoever I have commanded you: and, lo, I am with you always, even unto the end of the world"* (Matthew 28:19-20).

God has entrusted me with the awesome responsibility of raising my children in accordance with His Word. When they are older, and are challenged by the issues of life, they will not depart from what they were taught in their early years. Based upon what I have learned in this chapter, I will commit to raising my children in the following ways:

1. _____

2. _____

3. _____

4. _____

5. _____

Chapter Twenty-Three

Honor is Due!

"HONOUR THY FATHER AND MOTHER; WHICH IS THE
FIRST COMMANDMENT WITH PROMISE; THAT IT MAY BE
WELL WITH THEE, AND THOU MAYEST LIVE LONG ON
THE EARTH."
(Ephesians 6:2-3)

Until we become good children *of* God, we will never raise good children *for* God. God is our source, while parents are the resource with the awesome responsibility to raise God's children.

I fervently believe that our children will honor us, in accordance with God's Word, when they realize the value of a relationship with God, through Jesus Christ. This relationship comes through what we teach them when they are young. It is critical that we teach them:

Children must know that God is real.

We are to be in His image and in His likeness. They will not obey us if we do not obey God.

Children must know that God has an Unchanging Nature.

They must know that He is, He was, and He will be. To help them achieve this knowledge, we must have a consistent lifestyle.

Children must know that life is based upon choices.

If the choices are Godly, there is life. If the choices are ungodly, there is death and destruction.

"Honour" is mentioned 142 times in *The Holy Bible*. Other variations of this word include:

> ➤ Honourable – 30 times,
>
> ➤ Honoured – 10 times,
>
> ➤ Honourest – Once,
>
> ➤ Honoureth – 8 times, and
>
> ➤ Honours – Once.

In its original Greek form – *timē* – it is a noun that means "a valuing." In other forms, it means glory – *doxa*. As a verb, it means "to honor" – *timaō*. Similarly, in its original Hebrew dialect – *kābēd* – honour means to "to honor." This verb is used 114 times and in all periods of biblical Hebrew.

Be An Example to the Children

"One that ruleth well his own house, having his children in subjection with all gravity..."
(1 Timothy 3:4)

Ruleth well his own house means that he manages his family rightly. Having his children in subjection means that he brings about with all gravity (in a dignified manner) obedience by his children.

Children are motivated to honor their parents as a direct result of cherished memories from the past. Based upon what I have learned in this chapter, my children will honor me (us) later in life, based upon the deposit that I (we) left in their lives, because of the following:

1.

_____

2.

_____

3.

_____

4.

_____

5.

_____

Afterword

Prayerfully, *The Godly Family Life* has revealed some of the reasons why the family, as God intended, is out of balance and dangerously impacted. Man's open defiance to God's plan for his life is the direct result of the calamity that is presently before us. God spoke clearly through His servant Moses to the children of Israel as they prepared to enter the Promised Land, more than 4,000 years ago:

> *"I call heaven and earth to record this day against you, that I have set before you life and death, blessing and cursing: therefore choose life, that both thou and thy seed may live."* (Deuteronomy 30:19)

And, he is speaking to us today. His consistency is captured throughout *The Holy Bible* as a God who will not change:

He cannot change - *"For I am the Lord, I change not..."* (Malachi 3:6),

He cannot lie - *"That by two immutable things, in which it was impossible for God to lie..."* (Hebrews 6:18), and *"In hope of eternal life, which God, that cannot lie, promised before the world began"* (Titus 1:2),

177

He is the same forever - *"Jesus Christ the same yesterday, and to day, and for ever"* (Hebrews 13:8),

He cannot speak empty words - *"So shall my word be that goeth forth out of my mouth: it shall not return unto me void, but it shall prosper in the things whereto I sent"* (Isaiah 55:11), and

He cannot break any promises - *"My covenant will I not break, nor alter the thing that is gone out of my lips"* (Psalm 89:34).

As we read news stories, newspaper clippings, magazine articles, and view the non-stop bombardment of alternate lifestyle images on television and movie theaters, we must remember that God's plan for us and our intended role in our respective families is superior to man's thoughts. *Nearer My God To Thee*, U.S. News and World Report, May 3, 2004, page 59, is a recent news story that typifies how some Christians share similar views as mainstream Americans on subjects such as allowing gays to marry legally, political affiliations, abolishing gay marriage by amending the U.S. Constitution, and have enough muscle to influence American society. The more that we are exposed to this worldly system, the more we tend to behave in a manner that is contrary to God's Word.

Study the 23 chapters carefully. Spend quality time reviewing your answers to the five questions at the end of each chapter. God's Word can and will change your life and your personal perspective on His plan for your life.

Embrace it, live it, breathe it, and, more importantly, fulfill your role in your family. In doing so, you will leave a deposit in this world for the next generation, in accordance with God's will (Genesis 1:28).

Concluding Prayer

Heavenly Father, I come to you, in the precious name of Jesus, even the Christ, whose I am and whom I serve. Thank you, Father, for the privilege and opportunity to be used by You to share Your Word concerning the state of the family. It is my heart's desire to encourage, motivate, inspire, and educate my readers about the value of family, as You intended before the foundation of the world. I ask that You continue to grant me the desires of my heart as well as the fortitude and enthusiasm to spread the gospel of Jesus through this book series to the uttermost parts of the world, as I seek first the kingdom of God and Your righteousness.

Father, I ask that You move upon the hearts of the readers of this book with Your unconditional love, affectionate power, and amazing grace. Teach the men how to be Godly husbands and fathers. Teach the women how to be Godly wives and mothers. Teach the young people how to obey their parents and to stay under authority that will protect their lives. Help them to convert their ways so that they have a desire to apply biblical principles within their respective homes, in the name of Jesus. I ask that new illuminations and insight pierce their inner being so that they will desire to be transformed by the renewing of their minds.

I ask that the information contained within this book be used to glorify Your name, Father. I ask that families be restored and strengthened, that loved ones be reunited, that lives be saved and improved, that marriages acknowledge their vows unto You, and that the sanctity of family life be reenergized. It is in Jesus' name that I pray and give thanks. A-men.

APPENDIX A – *A Family Prayer*

APPENDIX B – *Case Law That Has Eroded the Family*

APPENDIX C – *10 Ways to Be a Better Dad*

APPENDIX A

A Family Prayer
by Kevin Wayne Johnson
© 2005

Heavenly Father, I come to you in the name of Jesus
What a joy I have today
To pray unto you
As I do each and every day.

As I wake each day at dawn
To a sun that you caused to rise,
I am again thankful for the opportunity
To have been welcomed into the body of Christ.

I pray for my family, Lord
Whom you created just for me
Your Word says to serve and provide for them
And to encourage them to be what your Word calls them to be.

I pray Father that my family will
Prosper, and be in good health, even as our souls prosper
And that we continually acknowledge You in all of our ways,
Knowing that You shall direct our paths that no one can conquer.

I pray for salvation and academic excellence
For each and every child today
And for my spouse, I pray for peace
That will never fade or away.

I pray Father that our beautiful family
Be a visible example in the earth
Of what Your Word teaches us
That is, to be a blessing and not a curse.

In exchange for Your love toward us
We promise this to you
That this family will remain intact
No matter what the world may say or do.

This family will boldly reflect
What your Word intends for the family to be,
A strong and loving father, a tender and caring mother,
And children who honor their parents as their authority.

Thank you, Father for the stewardship
That comes with parental accountability,
What a privilege to be trusted
With such responsibility!

Father, use our family
To make a change in society
To demonstrate Your awesome love
For all humanity.

Your Word says,
"Train up a child in the way that he should go,
So that when he is old, he will not depart from it."
We pledge to do this so our children won't be tossed to and fro.

Your Word teaches the man
To love his wife as Christ also loved the church
For she is his glory, as is to be regarded
As precious as Your only Sons' birth.

So Father, we touch and agree
Right now as we prepare for Your work today,
That Jesus is the solid rock upon which we stand
Even as You care for us every step along the way.

We pray for all families throughout our land
That they will come to know Your unconditional love,
And that Your original plan for the family
Will transcend all that is wrong with this world.

In Jesus' Name, Amen.

APPENDIX B

Case Law that has Eroded the Family:
Nine Landmark United States decisions that have undermined Christian values and the family

1. *June 17, 1962* – **Engel vs. Vitale**. The Supreme Court restricts prayer in schools.

2. *January 22, 1973* – **Roe vs. Wade**. The Supreme Court finds that the right to personal property includes abortion.

3. *November 17, 1980* – **Stone vs. Graham**. The Supreme Court strikes down a Kentucky statute requiring display of the Ten Commandments in public schools.

4. *June 30, 1994* – **Madsen vs. Women's Health Center**. The Supreme Court upholds the creation of so-called "buffer zones" around abortion clinics, severely restricting pro-life free speech.

5. *June 19, 2000* – **Santa Fe Ind. School District vs. Doe**. The Supreme Court overrules a Texas law allowing high school students to pray at athletic events.

6. *June 26, 2003* – **Lawrence vs. Texas**. The Supreme Court strikes down a Texas law prohibiting sodomy.

7. *July 1, 2003* – **Glassroth vs. Moore**. The 11th Circuit Court of Appeals rules that a monument to the Ten Commandments placed in Alabama's judiciary building must be removed, setting the stage for a Supreme Court showdown.

8. *November 6, 2003* – **Federal judges** in New York and California issue temporary restraining orders blocking enforcement of the Partial-Birth Abortion Ban Act.

9. *November 18, 2003* – **Goodridge vs. Department of Public Health**. The Massachusetts Supreme Court rules that same-sex couples can marry under the laws of that state.

Source: Focus on the Family, Colorado Springs, CO

187

APPENDIX C

10 Ways to Be a Better Dad

1. Respect Your Children's Mother

One of the best things a father can do for his children is to respect their mother. If you are married, keep your marriage strong and vital. If you're not married, it is still important to respect and support the mother of your children. A father and mother who respect each other, and let their children know it, provide a secure environment for them. When children see their parents respecting each other, they are more likely to feel that they are also accepted and respected.

2. Spend Time with Your Children

How a father spends his time tells his children what's important to him. If you always seem too busy for your children, they will feel neglected no matter what you say. Treasuring children often means sacrificing other things, but it is essential to spend time with your children. They grow up so quickly. Missed opportunities are forever lost.

3. Earn the Right to be Heard

All too often the only time a father speaks to his children is when they have done something wrong. That's why so many children cringe when their mother says, "Your father wants to talk to you." Begin talking with your children when they are very young so that difficult subjects will be easier to handle as they get older. Take time and listen to their ideas and problems.

4. Discipline with Love

All children need guidance and discipline, not as punishment, but to set reasonable limits. Remind your children of the consequences of their actions and provide meaningful rewards for desirable behavior.

5. Be a Role Model

Fathers are the role models to their children whether they realize it or not. A girl who spends time with a loving father grows up knowing she deserves to be treated with respect by boys, and what to look for in a husband. Fathers can teach sons what is important in life by demonstrating honesty, humility and responsibility. *"All the world's a stage..." and a father plays one of the most vital roles.*

6. Be a Teacher

Too many fathers think teaching is something others do. But a father who teaches his children about right and wrong, and encourages them to do their best, will see his children make good choices. Involved fathers use everyday examples to help their children learn the basic lessons of life.

7. Eat Together as a Family

Sharing a meal together (breakfast, lunch or dinner) can be an important part of healthy family life. In addition to providing some structure in a busy day, it gives children the chance to talk about what they are doing and want to do. It is also a good time for fathers to listen and give advice. Most importantly, it is a time for families to be together each day.

8. Read to Your Children

In a world where television often dominates the lives of children, it is important that fathers make the effort to read to their children. Children learn best by doing and reading, as well as seeing and hearing. Begin reading to your children when they are very young. When they are older encourage them to read on their own. Instilling your children with a love of reading is one of the best ways to ensure they will have a lifetime of personal and career growth.

9. Show Affection

Children need the security that comes from knowing they are wanted, accepted and loved by their family. Parents, especially fathers, need to feel both comfortable and willing to hug their children. Showing affection every day is the best way to let your children know that you love them.

10. Realize that a Father's Job is Never Done

Even after children are grown and are ready to leave home, they will still look to their fathers for wisdom and advice. Whether it's continued schooling, a new job or a wedding, fathers continue to play an essential part in the lives of their children as they grow and, perhaps, marry and build their own families.

Source: The National Fatherhood Initiative gives tips on improving your fatherly role (reprinted in the June/July 2004 issue – The New Birth Voice). *The author has replaced the term "kids" with children, as appropriate.*

Endnotes

1. Pastor John A. Cherry, "The Family Man" series, From the Heart Church, Temple Hills, MD, 1991 and 2003.

2. Rick Warren. *The Purpose Driven Life – What on Earth Am I Here for?* (Grand Rapids, MI: Zondervan, 2002), 117.

3. Pastor Frederick K.C. Price, Ever Increasing Faith Ministries monthly newsletter, Los Angeles, CA, August 2004.

4. Wade F. Horn, Ph.D. and Tom Sylvester. *Father Facts 4* (Gaithersburg, MD: National Fatherhood Initiative, 2002).

5. *US News & World Report*, (December 27, 2004 – January 3, 2005), 36.

6. Men's Fellowship monthly meeting, From the Heart Church, Inc., Temple Hills, MD, 2004.

7. Dr. James Dobson. *Bringing Up Boys* (Wheaton, IL: Tyndale House Publishers, Inc., 2001), 53.

8. William Owens. *Divine Protocol – The Order of God's Kingdom* (Kennesaw, GA: Higher Standard Publishers, LLC, 1998), 48.

9. Wade F. Horn, Ph.D. and Tom Sylvester. *Father Facts 4* (Gaithersburg, MD: National Fatherhood Initiative, 2002).

10. Dr. James Dobson. *Bringing Up Boys* (Wheaton, IL: Tyndale House Publishers, Inc., 2001), 60.

11. Pastor John A. Cherry, "Save the Seed" series, From the Heart Church, Temple Hills, MD, 2003.

12. Michel A. Bell. *Managing God's Time* (Enumclaw, WA: WinePress Publishing, 2004), 129.

13. Wade F. Horn, Ph.D. and Tom Sylvester. *Father Facts 4* (Gaithersburg, MD: National Fatherhood Initiative, 2002).

14. *Focus on the Family®* monthly magazine, February 2005, 26.

15. *The Holy Bible*, The New Open Bible Study Edition, King James Version Study Bible (Nashville, TN: Thomas Nelson Publishers, 1990), 6.

16. *The Holy Bible*, The New Open Bible Study Edition, King James Version Study Bible (Nashville, TN: Thomas Nelson Publishers, 1990), 219.

17. Robin Elise Weiss, LCCE. *A Birth Plan.*

18. 4Woman.gov, The National Women's Health Information Center Website

19. Dr. James Dobson. *Marriage Under Fire* (Sisters, OR: Multnomah® Publishers, 2004), 21.

20. Pastor John A. Cherry. *The Seven Spiritual Principles®*, From the Heart Church, Inc., Temple Hills, MD

21. Dr. James Dobson. *Marriage Under Fire* (Sisters, OR: Multnomah® Publishers, 2004), 17.

22. Webster's II New Riverside University Dictionary, The Riverside Publishing Company, 1984.

23. Pastor John A. Cherry. *The Seven Spiritual Principles®*, From the Heart Church, Inc., Temple Hills, MD

24.   Dr. James Dobson. *Marriage Under Fire* (Sisters, OR: Multnomah® Publishers, 2004), 18.

25.   *The Holy Bible*, The New Open Bible Study Edition, King James Version Study Bible (Nashville, TN: Thomas Nelson Publishers, 1990), 719.

Selected Bibliography and Recommended Reading

A Dictionary of Quotations from The Bible, Selected by Margaret Miner and Hugh Rawson (NY: Penguin Group (A Signet Book), 1990).

Banister, Doug, Fray, Jeff, Secrest, John, and Hall, Steve. *We're All in The Family Business* (Kingston, TN: Warren and Warren, Inc. in conjunction with TFB Publishing, 2004).

Bell, Michel A. *Managing God's Time* (Enumclaw, WA: WinePress Publishing, 2004).

Christian Parenting Today magazine, "Going Public (How to make the most of your child's Public School experience)," by Sheila Wray Gregoire, Fall 2003.

Christianity Today.com editorials, *Why It Takes a Man and a Woman*, January 30, 2005.

Davis, Bryan. *Spit and Polish for Husbands - Becoming Your Wife's Knight in Shining Armor* (Chattanooga, TN: AMG publishers, 2004).

Dobson, James Dr. *Focus on the Family* Newsletter.

Dobson, James Dr. *Focus on the Family* magazine.

Dobson, James Dr. *Bringing Up Boys* (Wheaton, IL: Tyndale House Publishers, Inc., 2001).

Dobson, James Dr. *Marriage Under Fire* (Sisters, OR: Multnomah ® Publishers, 2004).

Dockery, Karen, Godwin, Johnnie, Godwin, Phyllis. *The Student Bible Dictionary* (Uhrichsville, OH: Barbour Publishing, Inc., 2000).

Focus on the Family Action, Focus Action newsletter.

Focus on the Family® Marriage Series, *The Masterpiece Marriage.* Foreword by Gary Smalley (Gospel Light, 2003).

Focus on the Family® Marriage Series, *The Surprising Marriage.* Foreword by Gary Smalley (Gospel Light, 2003).

Horn, Wade F., Ph.D. and Sylvester, Tom. *Father Facts 4* (Gaithersburg, MD: National Fatherhood Initiative, 2002).

Lifelines magazine, Bethany Christian Services, Grand Rapids, MI.

New Man magazine, "When God Shines His Light," by Jonathan Edwards, July/August 2004.

Owens, William. *Divine Protocol – The Order of God's Kingdom* (Kennesaw, GA: Higher Standard Publishers, LLC, 1998).

RBC Ministries, *Our Daily Bread – For Personal and Family Devotions.*

RBC Ministries, *What Does God Expect of a Man?*

RBC Ministries, *What Does God Expect of a Woman?*

Strong, James. *Strong's Exhaustive Concordance of the Bible* (Peabody, MA: Hendrickson Publishers).

The Holy Bible, The New Open Bible Study Edition, King James Version Study Bible (Nashville, TN: Thomas Nelson Publishers, 1990).

The King James Study Bible, King James Version (Nashville, TN: Thomas Nelson Publishers).

The Vine newspaper, "The Anniversary of Homosexual Bishop's Confirmation Nearing," by Jim Brown, Agape Press, August 2004.

USA Today Newspaper.

U.S. News & World Report. *Nearer My God to Thee,* May 3, 2004, by Jeffrey L. Sheler.

U.S. News & World Report. *The Rise of the Gay Family,* May 24, 2004, by Dan Gilgoff.

U.S. News & World Report, *How We Talk to God,* December 20, 2004, by Marianne Szegedy-Maszak.

Vines, W.E., Unger, Merrill F., White, William, Jr. *Complete Expository Dictionary of Old and New Testament Words* (Nashville, TN: Thomas Nelson Publishers, 1984, 1996).

Warren, Rick. *The Purpose Driven Life – What on Earth Am I Here for?* (Grand Rapids, MI: Zondervan, 2002).

About the Author

Kevin is the eldest son of Ernest and the late Adele Johnson. Raised in Richmond, Virginia, he attended and graduated from Richmond Public Schools and Virginia Commonwealth University.

He is a 20-year veteran of the federal government and corporate America in the career field of contracting and procurement. Kevin's true love is for God. He confessed Jesus Christ as his personal Lord and Savior on May 2, 1993, alongside his wife Gail. This spiritual transformation occurred slightly less than two months after their marriage on March 6, 1993.

He and his wife are ordained deacons. He is a graduate of the True Disciple Ministries Bible Institute, Somerville, New Jersey, and he is also an adjunct faculty member at the National Bible College and Seminary in Fort Washington, MD.

Kevin currently lives in Clarksville, Maryland, with his wife, Gail, and their three young sons, Kevin, Christopher, and Cameron. He is the author of the nine-book series entitled *Give God the Glory!*, a recipient of multiple literary awards, and has hosted a talk show entitled *Give God the Glory!* on the VoiceAmerica Internet Talk Radio Network during the 2004 season. He is the current host of the *Give God the Glory!* television show on www.blacktvonline.com, which airs weekly on Tuesdays. He attests every day that God *uses ordinary people to accomplish extraordinary things!*

By: Kevin Wayne Johnson, Author of the *Give God the Glory!* series of books and devotional

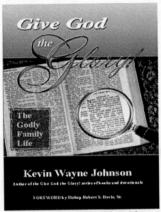

Book #4 in the *Give God the Glory!* series
Religion/Christian Living/Spirituality/Family/Relationships
ISBN: 0-9705902-3-7
978-0-9705902-3-8
Trade Paperback / 200 pages
Retail Price: $13.00 U.S. / $18.00 Canada
Dimensions: 6" x 9"
Publisher: *Writing for the Lord* ™ Ministries
Distributor: Faithworks, a division of Send the Light, Ltd.

Full Name: _____

Street Address: _____

City: _____ State: ____ Zip Code: _____

Telephone Number: _____Fax number: _____

1) Payment Options: Check __ Money Order __
   MasterCard ___ Visa ___

2) For credit cards orders, sign here and include the three-digit security code (on back of card):
Card Number _____Expiration Date _____

Security Code _____ Signature _____

3) On-line bookstore at – http://shop.writingforthelord.com and use PAYPAL: kgj2@att.net

**Mail payments and make checks/money orders payable to:
Writing for the Lord ™ Ministries, 6400 Shannon Court, Clarksville, MD 21029

Know therefore this day, and consider it in thine heart, that the LORD he is God in heaven above, and upon the earth beneath: there is none else.

(Deuteronomy 4:39)